THE GIFT
of
CRISIS

PRAISE FOR
THE GIFT OF CRISIS

"Bridgitte's writing comes directly from the heart, and will help you unblock your connection to your inner guidance."

–Elizabeth Lesser, co-founder of Omega Institute

"In a clear and compassionate style, Bridgitte Jackson-Buckley shows us the gift of both crisis and meditation–to lead us into our deepest wisdom and highest self. An evolved, insightful and genuinely helpful read!"

–Nancy Colier, psychotherapist, interfaith minister, author of *The Power of Off: The Mindful Way to Stay Sane in a Virtual World*

"What Bridgitte reminds us is that it is so important to continue the work that is ours to do, to push on, to be relentless, to be unfailingly loyal to ourselves and our higher being. She teaches that following our way requires persistence, repetition, and devotion. That being inspired and being fired by the passion within us is what is required to consistently apply the tools that we have, to gain our own level of enlightenment, our own bliss. Often self-help books try to tell us that we can do the work in a very easy way and get results instantly. What Bridgitte shows us is that it is not necessarily that the way itself that is difficult, but that we must be persistent in our practices, and this is what requires effort– ongoing and repeated effort."

–B. Jean Lein, CPA, ALSP, Certified Energy Codes Facilitator and Licensed Practitioner

"Bridgitte Jackson-Buckley has written an engaging story about how she integrated her spiritual self with her worldly personality to shift what I often call the 'inner blueprint'—that pattern of thought and energy that gives rise to physical reality. She used many creative perceptual methods to recreate her life to include more flow, supply, support, opportunity, and synchronicity. She demonstrates clearly how anyone can do it! It's a simple matter of changing your perception and frequency—really!"

—Penney Peirce, author of *Transparency, Leap of Perception,*
and *Frequency*

"Bridgitte Jackson-Buckley has the gift of observing the little details that make her story come to life, and make her spiritual journey meaningful. In her quest for a better way to live, she made discoveries of deep principles that will enrich your understanding of how the universe works. With careful attention to the step-by-step process she went through to get in touch with her inner guidance system, she provides a clear roadmap for clarifying your own thinking about your life, your potential, and your destiny."

—Chris Vogler, screenwriter, author of *The Writer's Journey*

"I had the pleasure of meeting Bridgitte Jackson-Buckley last year. During our conversation, we agreed that hard times can provide great opportunities to recapitulate what you have done, right or wrong, and where change is needed. With the wisdom and experience of someone who has done it in her own life, in *The Gift of Crisis*, Bridgitte offers amazing information to put movement toward change."

—Sergio Magaña Hidalgo, author of *Caves of Power: Ancient Energy Techniques for Healing, Rejuvenation and Manifestation*

"There is nothing more beautiful than a human story of awakening. To hear the direct experience of others, told with candor and heart, is a great teacher for us all. This is a touching, well-written and captivating account of one woman's life and if you read it you will get a sense of how one can be guided by some form of higher intelligence, if one starts to listen. However, dues must be paid. Bridgitte Jackson-Buckley paid them, and now lives from a deeply connected place in service to life."

–Megan McFeely, producer and director of *As She Is*

"In *The Gift of Crisis*, Bridgitte reveals very personal struggles and shares how she resolved them with guidance from her 'Higher Mind.' In a detailed, well-written account, the author shares how meditation practice shed new light and perspective on reoccurring challenges. The reader is encouraged to 'try this at home."

–Catherine Yunt, MC

"This book reminds us of the grace in the crisis, and the opportunity to transform and accept it as catalyst to live into our highest vision of our authentic life."

–Sande Hart, Director of the Charter for Compassion International
Women and Girls

THE GIFT
of
CRISIS

How I Used Meditation to Go from
Financial Failure to a Life of Purpose

Bridgitte Jackson-Buckley

Mango Publishing

CORAL GABLES

Cover & Layout Design: Jermaine Lau

For permission requests, please contact the publisher at:
Mango Publishing Group
2850 Douglas Road, 3rd Floor
Coral Gables, FL 33134 USA
info@mango.bz

For special orders, quantity sales, course adoptions and corporate sales, please email the publisher at sales@mango.bz. For trade and wholesale sales, please contact Ingram Publisher Services at customer.service@ingramcontent.com or +1.800.509.4887.

The Gift of Crisis: How I Used Meditation to Go from Financial Failure to a Life of Purpose

Library of Congress Cataloging
ISBN: 978-1-63353-794-1
Library of Congress Control Number: 2018952304
BISAC category code: BUS046000–BUSINESS & ECONOMICS/Motivational

Printed in the United States of America

To my loves:
Dennis, Greyson, Mckenna & Gavin
It is all always for you.

To my parents:
Matthew & Bobbie
For unconditional love that let me find my own way.

And to you, dear reader:
Be with your heart.

TABLE OF CONTENTS

FOREWORD

Sometimes a book title is all you need. The words on the cover grab you by the heart and won't let you go. *The Gift of Crisis* is such a title.

Crisis? Oh yeah, that's me. And it's you, too. It's everyone. Show me the person who hasn't been swept into the riptide of crisis. But it's the word Gift that made me open this book and, I must tell you, I opened it with a smile. I know this gift. I carry an armload of these gifts. Like Bridgitte Jackson-Buckley, I have faced a crisis or two or three. And each one, awful as it was at the time, handed me a gift to treasure for the rest of my life.

When you look at me, do you see an author? Radio host? How about a prayer artist or field guide in the mystic? I may be all those things, but look again, because when you look at me, you are looking at a poster child for the gifts of crisis. None of these lovely roles would ever have happened if I hadn't first lived through, and learned from, one life-shattering trauma after another. I am who I am because crisis came calling.

On page one, here's the most important thing I can tell you: It's not a crisis. It's a crossroads.

You can continue to walk the well-trod path of anger and blame. You know that road. You know that road all too well. You know how it feels and you know where it leads. Or you can turn your face directly into the wind and start walking down the unknown path, the one with no clear destination in sight.

If you do turn into the wind, here's what will happen. You will discover that the answers you so desperately seek are not outside you—and never were. They are the only place they can be—inside. And your broken heart is the perfect crack through which you can begin to draw them out. You'll start asking big, new questions—questions you've never considered. And you'll start listening. At first, the voice will seem small and you may not know exactly what you're hearing or who's speaking to whom. But you if you persist, you and your loving wise voice will build a relationship that overflows with trust and love. Then one day, the strangest thing will happen. You will find yourself once more on your knees, but this time you will have fallen to the ground with tears of gratitude for the crisis that taught you how to live.

Janet Conner, author of *Writing Down Your Soul, Soul Vows, Find Your Soul's Purpose* and more

INTRODUCTION

It is 10:30 p.m. on a clear, cool Saturday night in spring 2003. I sit on the sofa in the family room at my parents' house, folding warm clothes fresh out of the dryer. With the television blaring and the aroma of "Spring Delight" laundry freshener hovering in the air, I look at Dennis, who has fallen asleep in the recliner. He has been on alert since early this morning. Today is the day.

One by one I carefully fold pink blankets, yellow bibs, and light green burp cloths and place them into neatly arranged rows beside me on the sofa cushion. I look toward the laundry basket to make sure I have folded everything, and notice one light pink onesie laying on the rug beside my feet. These days leaning, walking, bending, getting up, and simply moving my belly around in the world is an effort. Long gone are the days of the cute basketball belly; my midsection has morphed into "globe" status. Before gravity gets the best of me, I lean to the side and quickly grab the onesie. I sit back on the sofa and, with arms outstretched, I hold the onesie in front of me. It can't be more than 10 inches long. With my head slightly tilted, I quietly look at the onesie and imagine the delicate life that will soon fill in all the empty spaces. For months, I've felt her move around inside the darkness of me slowly making her way into my world. "Who is she?" I wonder. I fold this last piece of clothing and place it in the bag for the hospital. Although I smile to myself, the wonder and excitement I feel is once again eclipsed by a slight trepidation. I'm not new to this. I have traveled this path once before. I know her arrival will be painful in more ways than one.

I know the unfathomable pain of bearing down to push a baby out of my body. I know the blanketed feelings of exhilaration and relief that come as soon as I release the baby and the pain entrenched in every muscle in my uterus. I know that, with the arrival of my new love, I will once again be thrust into the wanting of mothering; wanting full participation that will inevitably be interrupted due to financial responsibilities and work commitments. I also know that, as I relish the magic in the fleeting moments spent caring for her, it won't last, or at least not in the way I want it to.

Six years prior and with a completely different mindset, I had returned to California from my volunteer assignment in Honduras with the Peace Corps. I needed to do something, as in attend graduate school or get a full-time job. Upon my return, a good friend told me about the teacher shortage in California and that, because I am bilingual, I would be a good candidate for a teaching position. At that time, if you held a bachelor's degree, you could apply for work as an elementary teacher while attending school to obtain a teaching certification. I took my friend's suggestion and submitted my resume to the Santa Ana Unified School District on a Wednesday morning. Two days later, on Friday afternoon, I was employed as a first-grade bilingual teacher.

The quickness with which I was hired by the district led me to falsely believe this would always be the case; that as a job seeker I would be received well whenever I applied for work. I could not have been more wrong. This would turn out to be the first and last time that my resume and I would be accepted with such eager enthusiasm.

Throughout my first years as a teacher, I thoroughly enjoyed the engaged curiosity of my students, the creative aspects of instruction and the professional encouragement I received from the principal and my coworkers. At the close of the first semester of my second year of teaching, the students were reading, writing, and speaking English better than when they began the school year. I beamed with joy over the progress the students made throughout the year. The students could feel the pride I felt for them, not solely because of their improved test scores, but because of their continual effort. They worked hard, and they could see the results of their efforts as it reflected in their reading, writing, and speaking abilities.

However, despite moments such as this, I knew teaching wasn't something I would do for the rest of my life. Although I made notable progress in my first years of teaching, and was a well-regarded employee in previous professional positions, a restlessness lingered. Something was missing. Normally, I accept work positions that are a good fit as far as typical qualifications are concerned. However, no matter how well I carried out my work responsibilities, there continued to be an unnamable element missing; an internal longing that failed to subside, even in the best of professional situations. I knew I wasn't meant to stay here, nor would this be the last time I would feel this way.

It was near the end of my second year of teaching when I decided I had had enough of living and working in Orange County. As a black woman in Orange County, I felt invisible. Considering I'd lived in the OC off and on for almost ten years and had not been asked out on one date, enough was enough. It didn't take much for me to decide to relocate to the City of Angels–Los Angeles.

With so much diversity roaming about in LA, there is something, someplace, and someone for everybody. The only catch is, for all the good scenery, museums, weather, dating choices, and dance clubs, you pay dearly in the cost of living. I finished up my second year of teaching in Santa Ana and welcomed summer with a newly rented apartment in Los Angeles. Within a few weeks, I was hired by the Los Angeles Unified School District to continue as a first-grade bilingual teacher in the fall.

Living in LA afforded lots of opportunities for me to spend time with friends and meet new people. In keeping with my "someone for everybody in LA" perspective, that summer I was introduced to the man who would become the father of my three children, the man I would later marry, and the man with whom I would be compelled, through a series of unprecedented dire financial circumstances, to develop and usher in a new foundation for personal growth.

With his hands tucked away in his jeans pockets, he stood tall and quietly on the sidewalk and watched patiently as his childhood friend led my girlfriend and me over to meet him. The party was over and the outside late-night scene had just begun. This was the part of the night when final attempts were made and the excitement of the last romantic possibility was heightened. The three of us made our way through the crowd and stopped in front of him.

From the moment I was introduced to him, I felt an immediate return to love. I was drawn to him in a way that remained unknown. I felt as if I had known him all of my life. In his presence, I was intrigued, interested, and filled with the lightness of swirling butterflies. In the days and weeks that followed our introduction, I wanted to know everything about him. My head was trying to catch up to what was already known by my heart. Whenever we sat a dinner table together, walked through a park, watched the waves at the beach, laughed at silly personal stories, danced to our favorite Reggae music or simply lingered within the tenderness of each other, he attended to my every need with such endearing immediacy that I knew I was already loved.

At the time, the deeper aspects of our connection eluded me. I wasn't able to fully articulate what it was that so intensely drew me to him and him to me. What I have come to understand is we draw unto ourselves the very people, situations, and circumstances in which we share similar energetic vibrations and subconscious patterns. Of the millions of inhabitants of the LA dating scene, I managed to meet the one man with whom I would not only share an intense enduring love, but who would also mirror my deepest unexamined emotional wounds.

Unbeknownst to me, these unexamined emotional wounds that were buried so deeply within each of us would eventually rise to the surface. They would encompass our marriage, our home, our finances, and our way of perceiving and being in the world. They would also amplify the turmoil in which my most significant catalysts for personal growth would emerge. By the following summer, one year after I met Dennis, I was pregnant with our first child.

The news of "Bridgitte is pregnant" was met with hesitant excitement and spread like a thrilling rumor. First, with my decision to join the Peace Corps, and now, getting pregnant while unmarried, this was the second time I had done something that was unexpected and inconsistent with the normal trajectory of things. My parents were surprised, nervous, concerned, and happy all at once, as was I. However, they quickly became our most fervent supporters. We all agreed, married or not, a baby was indeed worthy of a celebration.

My mother, six of her closest girlfriends, and I planned our baby shower. We wanted to have a celebration that included all of our closest family and friends. By the time the event rolled around, we had more than 150 guests in attendance. For one of the game festivities, my stepfather, Matt, a football fanatic, agreed to create a Super Bowl Squares game that he would adapt for the baby shower. He used a poster board to create a ten-by-ten grid that would offer 100 squares for people to choose from. The rows indicated how many pounds I had gained during the pregnancy. The columns indicated the number of inches it would take to encircle my belly with a tape measure. When the guests were seated, Matt went around to each table, explained the game to everyone, and sold each square for five dollars. After everyone had purchased a square, all 100 squares were filled with names and we had five hundred dollars in the pot! Later that afternoon, during the game, I stood in front of the crowd as my mother pulled the tape measure around my midsection. We revealed the number of pounds I had gained and the circumference of my midsection. We then called the name located on the winning square and yelled, "Layla! You just won two hundred fifty dollars!" Dennis and I split the winnings with Layla, a friend of my mother. She was ecstatic and so were we.

Up until this point I still did not know the sex of the baby. When I had my six-months ultrasound, I requested that the technician write the sex of the baby on a piece of paper and seal it in an envelope. A few days after the ultrasound, I gave the envelope to my best friend, Nikki, to hold until the baby shower. We thought it would be a great idea to reveal the sex of the baby at the shower, and share the exciting news with everyone who had shown us so much love and support. During the baby shower and after the Super Bowl Squares game, we explained to our guests what we had done with the result of the ultrasound. When it was time to find out the sex of the baby, Dennis and I stood at the front of the room with everyone gathered in silent anticipation. Nikki reached into her purse, took out the small white envelope, walked to the front of the room, and handed it to Dennis. I stood to the side while my heart pounded with nervous anticipation. Dennis quickly ripped open the envelope, pulled out the tiny piece of white paper, and read the three words out loud that brought tears to my eyes. "It's a boy!" Laughter, cheers, and applause roared through the clubhouse as Dennis and I, along with our 150 guests, found out we would have a baby boy. The DJ turned up the music and those who were seated got out of their chairs and quickly moved onto the dance floor. Dennis held my hand as family and friends embraced us with an outpouring of love, joy, and well-wishes. It was one of the happiest moments of my life. By the end of the evening, we had received so many gifts that it took three separate trips, with the bed of my cousin's Ram pickup truck filled to capacity, to move all the gifts we received from the clubhouse up the hill to my parents' house. Neither Dennis nor I had ever experienced such tremendous generosity. We were overwhelmed with gratitude.

During the pregnancy, amidst all the excitement, I was filled with unanswered questions. I wondered about motherhood in general, how we would make the transition from "they're dating" to "they're parents," how we would afford quality childcare, who I would be comfortable with to provide childcare, and my life direction. How would I find my place in a world so vast that the act of making a choice had come to resemble a nightmarish paradox? I was scared to confront so much uncertainty. At that time, the two things I was certain of was that I was ready to become a mother and that Dennis and I equally wanted a child. I knew that, as an adult and self-sufficient woman, I was capable of taking on such an expansive responsibility. I was completely responsible for myself financially, and didn't ask for or need assistance. I was in a position to pay my living expenses in full and on time every month. Due to my ongoing love affair with Nordstrom's shoe department I wasn't, however, saving very much. Dennis worked in construction. He worked as an assistant to a general contractor and had plans to run his own contracting home improvement service. He wasn't making very much money, but I didn't feel much concern about his income because of what I earned. Surely I could handle diaper purchases, baby clothes, and round-the-clock breastfeeding. Surely I could forego my bi-weekly shoe purchase. Simply put, I knew I would be able to feed, house, and clothe the baby, and keep him alive.

After several information-filled question-and-answer discussions with my obstetrician and numerous late nights lying awake sifting through the pros and cons of the epidural, I decide to forego it. I want our child to begin life outside of my body with undiluted awareness. In hindsight, it was I who yearned for an undiluted sense of clarity and awareness. What will happen when this child enters my world? What unanticipated changes will he bring to my life? Who will he inspire me to become? Who will he become?

A month and a half after the baby shower, and on the exact date he is due, during what feels like the longest five minutes of my life, I push through excruciating pain without the aid of an epidural and give birth to our first child, Greyson.

Prior to the birth of Greyson, if anyone had tried to explain the profound ways in which becoming a mother can alter your perspective and change the course of your life, I don't think I would have fully understood. I don't think I would have been able to truly hear what was conveyed. I don't know that anyone can truly know the depth of change that can occur when you become a mother, until you actually live it. There was absolutely no question I wanted a child and this experience with Dennis. However, as far as the prior contemplation of the mental and emotional impact I would experience as result of bonding with my child, well, I didn't have many late nights lying awake in bed thinking about this one. I completely failed to give this crucial aspect of mothering the attention it deserves. It is within this breadth of failure that I would later find myself emotionally unprepared for separation from Greyson when it was time for my return to work.

I grew up in a household where the only option after high school that was ever discussed was to go to college. My parents encouraged my education and intellectual development with the utmost tenacity. I vividly remember my stepfather reiterating, "When you graduate from college and get a job, you should make no less than $1,500 per week." I had no perspective to grasp what making that type of income would entail. I remember the statement because it seared into my memory as my stepfather, with the best of intentions, vehemently defined what is to be my priority. Despite having spent much of my time as a child reading and writing in journals, and as a teenager writing articles for the high school newspaper, there was never any mention of the option or validity of doing creative work for a living; nor was there any mention of the possibility that, after giving birth, I might want to stay at home with my child. The notion of temporarily opting out of the professional workforce was never brought up, mentioned, discussed, or considered. The one piece of advice I do remember receiving from my mother was never to be dependent on a man.

The emotional transition I underwent to become a mother was intimately personal, and at times utterly unfamiliar. Although he was no longer inside my body, remnants of him remained untouched inside me. Through what felt like emotional osmosis, I immediately embraced my new role as the caregiver of this child that now engulfed my heart. With the presence of Greyson, maternal love awakened an unfamiliar primal devotion.

The months leading up to my return to work were nothing less than nerve-racking. Prior to my maternity leave, the principal at the school where I worked asked me four times if I would return to work after having the baby. The fact that she asked me so many times should have given me some clue as to what might happen. I was so sure I would return. In fact, I assured the principal I would return to work in the fall and dismissed her concern. However, four months after Greyson's birth, the new school year began, and I was not in my classroom. I couldn't leave him. For lack of a more explicit reason to justify going back on my word, it didn't feel right. It felt wrong. I couldn't bear the thought of the vulnerability I would subject Greyson to by placing him in the care of a stranger. I delayed going back to work for as long as I could, which essentially meant for as long as I could pay rent without having a monthly income. I was able to stay home with Greyson until he was eight months old. Since I didn't return to LAUSD, I had to find another teaching position. Thanks to the ongoing teacher shortage, I was able to sign on with the Hawthorne School District as a kindergarten teacher and began teaching in the spring. The new school was located literally five minutes from our apartment. The plan was for Dennis to stay home with Greyson during the day, bring him to the school during my lunch break so I could breastfeed, and go to work when I got home at 3:00 p.m. We maintained this rotation until Greyson was ten months old. When I found out my biological father's wife had a childcare service, we decided to make a change. Dennis was beginning to complain about how little he was able to accomplish with work on the current schedule. With hesitation, I agreed to let her watch Greyson.

For the most part, things seemed to be going okay with our new childcare arrangement. By now Greyson was almost eighteen months old. Then one afternoon, I arrived at my stepmother's house to pick up Greyson. I walked into the house as usual, and looked for Greyson. He was not there. My heart began to race. I quickly went to find my stepmother. She was in her room, talking on the phone. I politely interrupted, "Um, where is Greyson?" She said, "Oh, I sent him over to my sister-in-law's house because I had a headache." She spoke with the most casual tone, as if she had told me he was playing outside in the backyard. I looked at that woman like she had completely lost her mind and said, "What?" She said, "Oh, don't worry, she's really good with kids." Just try for a second to imagine how hard it was for me to stay calm at this point. I did not know her sister-in-law, nor have we ever discussed the option for Greyson to be sent to someone else's house without my consent. How did she come to the conclusion that this was a good choice? How many times has she done this without telling me? What else is going on that I'm not aware of? I was beside myself.

When I walked into her sister-in-law's dark apartment, Greyson was sitting on the couch with a busted lip and dried blood on his mouth. According to the sister-in-law, who did not speak English, which meant we had to do this entire exchange of information in Spanish, another child had thrown a bottle which hit Greyson on his lip. My Spanish was still intact, but imagine me standing in her living room/bedroom, holding Greyson, trying to stay calm, mentally translating what she was saying to me while trying to find the right words in Spanish to relay how angry I was. I took the rest of the week off from work and found a preschool that would accept Greyson immediately.

Preschool was an adjustment. Greyson had to get used to being around many different types of children and to the rules in a new setting, and I had to get used to the $775 monthly tuition payment for a child who could feed himself. After the experience with the sister-in-law, what choice did I have? Now, three years after the birth of Greyson, his sister was due the next day.

"Dennis," I call out. He has dozed off on the Lazy Boy with a pencil and the Contraction Count Card in his hands. "How many minutes ago was the last contraction?" I ask him. He has been timing the space between the contractions since this morning. The contractions haven't gotten any closer than an hour apart. Other than the sharp pain in my lower back earlier this evening, while we were out having dinner, and my protruding belly, there is no sign of her arrival. Then, all of a sudden, and I mean out of nowhere, I have to go to the restroom immediately! I quickly scoot to the edge of the sofa, brace my arms for support and push myself up. I make it into the bathroom just fine. However, as I finish using the bathroom and stand to straighten my clothes, a stabbing pain simultaneously shoots through the front of my uterus and lower back. The pain is so intense my knees buckle, and I fall down onto the floor! It feels like a sharp object has been lodged in my lower back. I try to catch my breath, but with continuous pain it is difficult to breathe. I reach up to grab the doorknob. Thank goodness I didn't lock it. I pull down on the doorknob. The door opens just enough to bump the top of my head. "Dennis!" A few feet away in the family room, he quickly comes around the corner and carefully squeezes through the bathroom door opening. "Is the baby coming? Can you stand? Did the water break?" he asks without pause. I can't answer. I grab onto his arm to try to get up when another jolt of pain stabs at my uterus. It is unbelievable. It's almost 11:00 p.m., the contractions are rapidly intensifying, and it is clear she is coming. Dennis pulls me up off the floor, and I take three steps before another jolt of pain hits again. Each time I have a contraction, I do the one thing you are advised not to do. I tighten e–v–e–r–y single muscle in my body. The Lamaze breathing techniques I practiced during my first pregnancy are difficult to remember, due to the shock of how quickly this is happening. Dennis calls out to my mother while holding me up to keep me from falling back to the floor. It takes fifteen minutes for Dennis and my mother to get me less than fifty feet, from the bathroom to Dennis' truck parked outside in the driveway. Once I am seated in the truck, Dennis runs around to the driver's side, jumps in, and quickly starts the engine. My mother gets into her car with Greyson and my brother, Christopher. The hospital is a ten-minute drive from my parents' house. My mother and Dennis carefully bypass red and green lights. I hold onto the door handle and squeeze so tightly my hand is numb. As soon as I catch my breath, another contraction. The contractions that were practically non-existent less than forty-five minutes ago are now less than five minutes apart and relentless. Finally, both cars come to a screeching halt at the Emergency Department entrance. Dennis jumps out of the car and runs inside to get a wheelchair. It's 11:35 p.m. I am immediately wheeled into a private room to get into a hospital gown. I can't tell what is going on with the nursing staff, but they are moving incredibly slowly. After several minutes, I am wheeled into a delivery room for the doctor's exam to determine the cervical dilation. At 11:50 p.m., the doctor lifts the sheet that covers me from the waist down. This time all thoughts of clarity and "clear beginnings" are out the door. I beg for the epidural. The pain is unbearable! The doctor quickly covers me back up with the sheet and responds, "You're way beyond medicine now!" The next thing I know, the nurses are scurrying around the room in preparation for an immediate delivery. The reason the pain is more intense this time is because she is already coming out! I'm not merely having contractions, my body is holding her inside! At 12:01 a.m. on March 30th, the exact day she is due, the doctor says, "Alright, Bridgitte! I need you to push as hard as you can and don't stop!" For the second time, I bear down with my remaining strength and push! At 12:10 a.m., Mckenna, our second child, is born.

After not wanting to leave Greyson, trying to find quality childcare that wasn't equivalent to the cost of a mortgage, and dealing with the discomfort of leaving a baby with someone in whom I did not have implicit trust, I decided to remain at home with my daughter instead of returning to work.

When I made this decision, the teacher shortage in California was beginning to wind down. Teachers who were employed on Emergency Teaching Credentials were being laid off. I was one of those teachers. After six years of teaching at the elementary level, I received my layoff notice two months after Mckenna was born. This meant I was eligible for unemployment benefits. With the little money I had saved while teaching, the unemployment benefits that would hopefully stretch out for six months or more, and Dennis securing more home improvement work projects, I felt optimistic. It appeared the stay-at-home situation with Mckenna might actually work. We didn't have a strong financial safety net in place, but, as I was able to identify potential income streams, I was determined to make it happen.

In a disturbing turn of events, two years later, Dennis was hospitalized due to the onset of symptoms for a stroke. He was thirty-three years old. When Dennis was admitted to the hospital, this completely changed the course of our lives. Every wheel that was turning forward stopped. In every way imaginable, we were unprepared to deal with the long-term effects of the mental, emotional, and financial challenges that lay ahead. The combination of financial distress, parental responsibilities, health crises, unexamined emotional wounds, blame, resentment, fear, and anger unearthed elements of our psyches that nearly destroyed us and our marriage. The loss of his ability to work propelled us into the beginning stage of what became the most prolonged and difficult period of our lives. For the next several years, we experienced the devastating loss of our home through foreclosure, ruptured familial relationships, job loss, and the steady decline of our marriage.

Throughout this period, there were repeated times when I thought I would not be able to go on; when I simply could not endure another minute of the mental and emotional despair in which I lived. For so long I believed myself to be the victim of these unwanted circumstances; that I was somehow being punished for past behaviors. It never occurred to me that the abysmal circumstances provided an invitation to move toward growth that can be garnered through challenge. It wasn't until I began sincere self-examination and contemplation, meditation, and prayer, all of which were encouraged in the self-help books I read, that I was ready to understand my role in creating crisis. You might be thinking, "It doesn't take a genius to realize the role one plays in creating problems in life." And you're right, it doesn't take a genius to identify where some problems stem from. However, there is a deeper side to perpetual problems, chaos, and crisis. There is a deeper, unconscious part of ourselves that heavily influences our choices, behaviors, beliefs, and feelings. The unexamined and unresolved aspects of the subconscious influence who we are and what we do. Meditation helped to clear the mental pathway for the issues to come into my awareness, into my conscious mind. As I sank deeper into prayer, meditation, surrender, and seeking clarity through asking for guidance, the light within the darkness slowly began to emerge.

"When the heart is ready for a fresh beginning, unforeseen things can emerge. And in a sense, this is exactly what a beginning does. It is an opening for surprises. Surrounding the intention and the act of beginning, there are always exciting possibilities. Such beginnings have their own mind, and they invite and unveil new gifts and arrivals in one's life. Beginnings are new horizons that want to be seen; they are not regressions or repetitions. Somehow they win clearance and become fiercely free of the grip of the past. What is the new horizon in you that wants to be seen?"

—John O'Donohue, *To Bless the Space Between Us*

When I was a child, my mother and I attended a Baptist church. I spent many Sunday afternoons sitting on an uncomfortable wooden pew, listening to sermons about the strong possibility of my going to hell. At twelve years old, I even had a traditional water baptism. However, despite a religious background, at some point during the trying times of my adult life, I moved away from faith into fear and scarcity. I recall having made some major decisions rooted in fear, poverty mentality, and heavily disguised self-doubt, and, because of this, I did not always honor what was in my heart. The more I let fear take the lead in how to direct my life, the closer I moved toward crisis.

After years of prolonged financial problems, I had to accept that I could no longer ignore the repetition of these problems in my life. The crises in my life eventually served as catalysts to understand that I needed to make different choices to engage higher perspectives. In reading self-help and personal growth books, I began to understand that, when there is a recurring problem, such as the financial hardship we experienced, the underlying messages want to be revealed. They will make a continuous, unyielding effort to get our attention. The opportunity that lies within crisis is for you to be willing to look closely and identify the underlying patterns and messages in what is happening around you.

In the prolonged crisis, reading the books I read and listening to inspirational talks encouraged me to be still and quiet in order to allow the deeper messages to make themselves known. It was from this humble beginning that I actively began to participate in what would become my saving grace: going within to seek clarity through meditation and prayer.

Throughout the turmoil, it wasn't easy. With continual highs and lows, I began to tire of listening to myself whine and complain. Although I was scared and I wanted answers, I didn't want to continue to discuss our situation with family and friends. With no money to pay for therapy or counseling, it seemed the only place left for me to go was within. So I did.

During my meditations, in addition to periods of silence after prayer, I began to ask questions to solicit clarity and guidance into my awareness. As I posed questions during a meditative state, I began to notice answers would indeed come into my awareness. However, as soon as the meditation session was over, I forgot the guidance which came into my awareness. The only way to remember would be to write it down. It was at that time that I decided to bring a large pad and pen to my meditation and prayer sessions. At the start of the meditation, I would first pray, then move into a period of sustained silence. After getting comfortable for several minutes of complete silence, I was more relaxed, and thoughts that continued to hover would begin to fade. With my eyes closed, I would then say the following:

"I call upon my Higher Self to join me in my meditation. During this meditation, I ask that you protect me from any and all vibrations, energies, frequencies and communications in all directions of time past, present, and future, that are not of love, light, and the highest good. Please let this communication be clear. Let the answers be communicated to me in a way that is easy for me to understand. Please let me feel your loving energy when you are ready to begin. I thank you in advance for your presence."

For more than a year, I sat down in a meditative state to ask questions to help me mentally and emotionally navigate the difficult and uncertain times I faced. The guidance I recorded helped me to move through difficult and unsettling times with comforting reassurance that I am deeply loved, there is no need to be afraid, and I am not alone. The guidance I received, however, did not provide the answers I wanted. My posed questions and concerns were continual attempts to address the immediate unfavorable conditions which surrounded me. The guidance, however, provided the larger context of what was happening in my life and the higher messages that sought to make themselves known.

In the beginning, when I felt anxiety surrounding the outcome of a situation, I utilized my spiritual practice for a "save me please" answer. I wanted someone, something, anything to tell me what to do, to whom I should speak and what I should say. For a long period of time, I wanted to be rescued. I didn't want to do the "heavy lifting" of looking at what was underneath. In the beginning, when I began to ask for guidance, those times were no different. I didn't want anything vague. I wanted the final answer in the form of a deeply fulfilling (and immediate) job. However, that's not how this works. That's not how any of this works.

What is important to understand is that, for years, fear dominated my responses, choices, reactions, conversation, and movement throughout my life. I was consistently afraid that some event would occur that we would not be able to financially handle. Eventually it did. For a prolonged period of time, we could to not afford to live anywhere. We could not pay our bills. It was an unyielding struggle which took a toll on every aspect of our life. Before establishing a consistent meditation practice, I constantly felt threatened by a looming financial disaster. My nerves "lived" in fight-or-flight mode from the endless anxiety I created.

In the midst of this silent struggle, I turned within to be able to make it through each day. I knew I could either continue to do things as I always have, or take a chance of trusting my intuition and absorbing what the moment was trying to teach me. Life is not always linear, pretty, and clear. Sometimes you have to step outside of the box, especially when you're being pulled out of the box. With this in mind, I continued to meditate. Meditation grew to become the most practical, accessible, and effective way I found to calm myself of the anxiety-ridden thoughts that propelled me.

Let's be clear, meditation did not immediately remove any situation from my life. That's not what it does. Although mediation can be a powerful tool for personal growth, it is not a quick fix. What it did was help me establish, and strengthen, my practice as a way to move through the conundrum of situational difficulties with greater ease and trust, and a sense of growing empowerment. There were deeply held unconscious beliefs that were unknowingly contributing to the problems in my life; meditation helped to bring these unconscious beliefs to the surface to be consciously addressed and released.

Here are the three levels of the mind that influence our lives:

1. **The conscious mind** is everything you are aware of and thinking about.

2. **The subconscious mind** consists of accessible information you can become aware of once you direct your attention to it; memory recall.

3. **The unconscious mind** includes unconscious beliefs, patterns, feelings, thoughts, urges, and memories that are outside of our conscious awareness where information is hidden and stored. Most of these contents are unacceptable or unpleasant, such as feelings of pain, anxiety, or conflict, which trigger automatic reactions according to stored memories.

Within each of us there is also a higher part that goes beyond our conscious awareness. This Higher Self always has access to and communicates with a higher, more expansive and intelligent Divine Consciousness that some refer to as God, the I AM Presence or something else. The Higher Self is the highest expression of your individual connection with the Divine Consciousness. It is greater than our conscious everyday self. It is part of you, yet more than you. It is in and of itself a part of the Divine Consciousness. Within the practice of quieting the mind and connecting with your Higher Self, you can access unconscious information from the highest part of yourself that is out of your conscious awareness.

Meditation is the "doorway" through which I was able to quiet my mind and access unconscious information from my Higher Self. Through meditation, higher information can be brought into our conscious awareness to identify the best course of action towards the highest outcome.

Consciousness is the state or quality of awareness, or of being aware of something within oneself, it is your experience of awareness. By establishing a sincere and inquisitive connection with my Higher Self, I made myself available to receive help, to have a glimpse of what is possible through states of higher consciousness and essentially grow through challenges.

During this time of ongoing meditation, I still had moments of feeling afraid of what could go wrong. However, little by little, fear played a less significant role in my life. It took several years, in fact, of deeply sincere and active participation in meditation, prayer, introspection, and study to no longer be ruled by fear and self-sabotaging patterns. Simply put, I had a lot of "unlearning" to do. I had to make an effort to uncover the hidden parts of myself which kept me attached to financial disarray and problematic situations. Every time I sat down in silence to meditate and connect with my Higher Self, I knew I was not alone, my efforts to become a better expression of myself were not in vain, and my intentions were held in grace.

I began to notice the ways in which meditation helped me to become aware of the ways in which I blocked the clear flow of inner guidance with constant thinking and worry, and my resistance to let go of that which I said I no longer wanted. I also began to notice how grace appeared in my life in simple and small, yet miraculous, outcomes. For example, the willingness of the property owner to work with us when we were behind on rent payments, the manner in which I was led to the exact work situation and professional environment that served as "fertile soil" to enhance my personal growth, and the like-minded individuals I met along the way were but a few examples of how grace unfolded. These experiences, in the manner and time in which they occurred, pushed me to thoroughly examine my self-sabotaging habits, beliefs, emotional patterns, and ways of perceiving and being in the world. It was not pretty to look at the mess I had orchestrated, but, when you sincerely want change, you can no longer hide. You won't be allowed to hide because, in order to grow, you will have to take responsibility for everything in your life. Everything.

Now, years later, as I read the guidance, it makes perfect sense. I share this with you because I have come to see that although the guidance was pivotal for me and came through me, it is not solely meant for me. It is also meant for those who find themselves in similar situations of distress, and are open and willing to cultivate a connection with a higher consciousness to better discern where life is trying to lead them.

With repetition and simplicity, the guidance addressed the following themes of the human condition:

Holding a Vision	Whole-Heart Living	Living with Purpose
Healing	Love & Gratitude	Expansion of Consciousness
Forgiveness	New Beginnings	Transformation & Change
Mindfulness	Power of Prayer	Humility
Faith	Overcoming Fear	Personal Clarity

In addition to the loving energy I felt as the guidance came through, I began to feel a bit calmer each day. Over time, my mind began to interpret fewer situations as stressful. I was able to remain more centered and be less agitated by external events. I wasn't as susceptible to being emotionally triggered into a state of fear, anxiety, anger, impatience, sadness, or depression. I did still experience these emotions. However, I became less and less pulled around by them. There was less agony and, instead, more openness to new possibilities.

Knowing that we can see ourselves in the stories of others, it is my sincerest wish that the guidance from these meditations is as helpful to you as it has been for me. It is my wish that you will grow to trust yourself; that you will trust the inner guidance that is available and within you. It is my hope that you will seek out the opportunities for personal growth that lie in mundane and long-term struggles, and come to know that nothing we experience in this life is futile. With hindsight, it becomes clear that struggle and triumph both serve a higher purpose for personal growth. And finally, it is my greatest hope that you too will have the courage to let your crisis become the catalyst that ultimately leads you onto your highest life path. So often it is said that "meditation helps" until it almost seems like a redundant Hallmark-ish cliché. I can honestly say this is absolutely true. Meditation does help. Meditation can help.

CHAPTER ONE

THE HOUSE ON FORTY-FIRST

It began in a way many great ideas come about, over a dinner conversation; or at least what are hoped to be great ideas. It is a tranquil, sunny California afternoon. Dennis and I drive out to my parents' house for Sunday dinner and to pick up Greyson and Mckenna. From the start, my mother isn't merely interested in being Granny. She is interested in co-parenting. She wants to be a part of every single aspect of her grandchildren's lives, including supporting a single-family housing situation for them.

At the time, Dennis and I live in a two-bedroom apartment. We want to buy a house, but the housing prices in Los Angeles are out of control. A single-family home in LA would sell for close to $600,000, and would likely require major renovations!

Although Dennis is doing extremely well with work, and our income is close to $80,000, we know we won't qualify for a home loan. His credit history is okay, and mine consists of fickle "relationships" with Nordstrom, Citibank, Discover, and MBNA. Having been laid off two months after Mckenna was born, my income is one-third of my teacher's salary and has an end date. I am receiving unemployment, which is available for a specific amount of time. Although we are having a decent year with income, we need a stronger financial story to be approved for a home loan.

While at my parents' for dinner that afternoon, the inevitable conversation about the housing market and when we would purchase our first home comes up. Normally, I give Matt an *I'm-not-sure-so-don't-ask-me-any-questions* type of answer, but, for some reason, I speak candidly. He, along with my mother, raised me since I was in the second grade. He was my biggest intellectual advocate, always encouraging me. He knows what's going on with the housing market because this is what he loves to talk about—mortgages, interest rates, refinance rates, and home ownership—and today, I want to talk housing. Somewhere in between his explanation of the financial benefits of homeownership, the kids playing in the den, and Anderson Cooper's perpetual Breaking News report on the upcoming 2004 presidential election, my mother asks, "What about the house on Forty-first?"

The "house on Forty-first," as everyone in my family calls it, has been in our family for over twenty-five years. It is the first house my mother bought on her own as a young woman in the '70s. At the time, I was an only child, and lived in the house with my mother and grandmother for several years. On Forty-first, cousins my age would visit from Houston and Maryland to spend summers with us. I remember one summer night not being able to sleep because I was so excited to go to Disneyland with my cousins. I gave myself a stomachache from anticipation. And the milestone to surpass all childhood memories happened when my mother took me and my cousins, to the Cinerama Dome on Sunset Boulevard to see Star Wars for the first time. We were beside ourselves in our new movie clothes as we rode the escalator down to see Princess Leia, Luke, and Darth Vader!

My young-adult cousins in the LA area would stop by almost daily to see my mother and grandmother. We held family barbecues, Sunday dinners, welcomed neighbors as extended family members, witnessed family arguments and drunken rants between uncles and nephews, marriage break-ups, and births, and, from time to time, a visit from my grandmother's sister from Texas, while we lived in the house on Forty-first.

In addition to summer visits with my cousins, my fondest memories on Forty-first are of times with my grandmother. Her presence held our extended family together. While my mother worked, and within the leisure of an elderly person's routine, I spent ordinary days deepening the connection of love with my grandmother. Once a week, before 7:00 a.m., I peeked through the front bedroom window to watch her greet the neighborhood milkman, who delivered fresh milk in glass bottles to our doorstep in exchange for last week's empty bottles. She and I would often walk to G&J Market around the corner to buy thick-cut bacon and eggs. When we returned home from the market, she would soak the bacon for what seemed like hours in the kitchen sink, in a little soap and water. Later, the smell of fried bacon and eggs and baked biscuits drifted throughout the house while we sat at the kitchen table and ate a late breakfast. Afterward, in her favorite worn smock and slippers, she would shuffle through the kitchen holding a cup of coffee, while beginning lunch preparation for the inevitable visits from her sons and grandchildren, my uncles and cousins. On Forty-first, it was just us women. My biological father never lived with us. I have vague memories of waiting for him to pick me up, and of him leaning against his car in front of our driveway. He was never invited inside like everyone else. It wasn't until years later, on a morning walk with my mother, that she casually revealed a forgotten memory of how I used to wait for my father, who sometimes did not come when he said he would. Little did I know it would take years of crisis to spur the awakening necessary to work through the abandonment I came to associate with the simple act of waiting.

My mother and Matt still own the house after all these years, but rent it out to the daughter of a family friend we met when we moved in. The family friend, who rents the house, and I played together decades ago with the other kids on the street. One summer afternoon, several of us were outside playing and found an old pair of open handcuffs with no key. I can't recall whose great idea it was for me to put the handcuffs on my wrists, but I did. I put them on without the slightest consideration of how they would come off. Three hours later, after extended elementary deliberation, there was nothing we could do on our own. I couldn't tell my grandmother because she would have had a fit, *and* the streetlights were almost on! Most of the kids on the block had to be inside the house when the streetlights came on, so we had to get the cuffs off. At least ten of my friends walked me around the block to the neighborhood police station. I remember walking and crying on my way to the police station. Would they call my mother at work? Would my grandmother shuffle down to the station? She would have come down there alright, and none of us would have liked it. Fortunately, the police officer had a key to unlock the handcuffs, but he called my mother anyway.

When my mother suggests that Dennis and I buy the house on Forty-first from them, it is like a gift. They are willing to help us reach for something out of our reach. With the LA housing market pricing many inhabitants out of the market, this is our way in. And with Dennis' home improvement skills, he can manage the renovation of the house. The house is more than eighty years old and has been renovated once under my parents' ownership. That afternoon, my parents and I discuss the possibilities of the house at length:

what it needs, what Dennis can do, how we will find a realtor, where we will live during the renovation, and how they can legally inform the tenant she will have to move.

A few weeks later, Dennis, my parents and I meet with a realtor, who confirms what we suspect. Dennis and I do not qualify for a home loan. However, we still want to go ahead with the plan to move into the house. The agreement we settle upon is as follows:

With ample equity in the house, my parents will refinance the house and take out a loan to renovate it. Dennis and I will move our family in, and rent the house from my parents by paying the monthly mortgage while we work on our credit to qualify for a home loan to purchase it.

Dennis agrees to completely modernize the house. To do this, it will be have to be completely gutted. Dennis, with occasional hired help, will have to tear out everything in the house, down to the studs, floors, interior walls, and windows, the plumbing and electrical wiring.

To use the space differently with an open floor plan, Dennis has to move the gas line and reroute the plumbing to accommodate the relocation of the stove, dryer, and water heater. He insulates the walls before installing new drywall throughout the entire 1,214-square-foot house, then new wiring and new copper plumbing, and rearranges the bathroom to install a built-in deck for a drop-in bathtub, stand-up shower, new cabinets, and crown moldings. Who has crown moldings in the bathroom? We do! There are new countertops and appliances in the kitchen and an island, built-in closets in both bedrooms, a newly constructed deck added onto the back of the house, new central heating, newly installed floating laminate flooring throughout the entire house, and recessed lighting in the living room and kitchen, along with a new gate to the back yard and newly planted flowers near the front porch. The demolition and reconstruction are extensive and take almost a year. For that year, we live with my parents and pay the mortgage on the house on Forty-first. Dennis completes a lot of the work on the house on weekends and sometimes after work. He saves us a fortune on labor, planning, and installation costs, and does absolutely beautiful work on the house.

In June 2005, we move out of my parents' house into our beautiful new home with superb water pressure, no exposure to lead paint dust or chips, clear windows, a long driveway, and a spacious backyard for the kids to play freely. Three months later, in September 2005, after two children and seven years of being together, Dennis and I are married amongst sixty-five of our closest family and friends in my parents' backyard. The details of my life with Dennis, Greyson, and Mckenna resemble perfection. Everywhere I look there is something beautiful to see.

In an unexpected turn of events, six months after moving into the house and three months after the wedding, the attempt to grasp our version of the American Dream slips away like the sun disappears below the horizon. In December 2005, Dennis is hospitalized due to the onset of symptoms for a stroke. He is thirty-three years old.

There is nothing unusual about that Tuesday afternoon, other than that, after picking Greyson up from school, I have a strong feeling I should go straight home. Usually, after school, I would stop at the park or library instead of going home. But, on this day, my intuition pulls at me to go home without delay. Instead of pulling into the backyard, closing the gate behind the car and entering the house through the back door as usual, I pull halfway up the driveway and enter through the front door. When I open the door, Dennis is sitting on the couch. He's moaning and holding his head in severe pain. "What's wrong?!" I ask and kneel down in front of him. "I have the worst headache I've ever had in my life." I will never know why I don't hesitate, but I tell Greyson and Mckenna to get back into the car. I help Dennis get up to walk outside and get into the car. I drive as fast as I can to Hubert Humphrey Comprehensive Health Center, where his sister, with whom I rarely speak, is the head nurse. As soon as we walk into the clinic, Dennis begins to vomit repeatedly. His sister is working there that day and sees us. She takes Dennis to the back immediately. The next thing I know, I hear the ambulance's siren as it pulls up to the center. His sister comes out from behind the counter, over to me, and says, "His blood pressure is 220/180; he has to be admitted to the hospital right now! You can meet him there! I hope he doesn't have retinal separation!" When I walk into the Emergency Department at LA County USC and say, "I'm here for Dennis Buckley," three nursing students, who stand by the intake counter stare at me in wide-eyed silence. My chest wants to explode. What do their looks mean?! A nurse leads me to the room where Dennis lie writhing on the hospital bed, still moaning in pain. There are so many wires attached to him. I call out to him, but he keeps asking, "Who are you?!" He can't see me. He has lost his vision. I stand motionless with Mckenna on my hip, Greyson crying at my side, and the nurse prodding me for information: "Are you his wife? How long has he been like this? Did he hit his head? Did he complain of numbness? How old is he?" The room is spinning for me and for Dennis. It takes all my bearings to remain standing upright. I nod yes to being the wife. There are two nurses and a doctor standing around the bed. One nurse is looking at the heart monitor while the doctor shines light onto Dennis' pupils and loudly calls his name. Again, the nurse asks, "Mrs. Buckley? Did he hit his head?" My eyes blink slowly. Greyson holds onto my arm, and minutes of standing in the room feel like hours. I can barely think logically, let alone answer questions. What the hell is happening?

Five hours later, the doctor explains Dennis was on the verge of having a stroke due to untreated hypertension. The rapid rise in blood pressure to extremely high levels can cause immediate and potentially deadly damage to systems in the body; therefore, he will have to remain hospitalized to slowly bring down his blood pressure over a period of days. His vision will slowly return. The weight of Mckenna's limp body on my hip feels like a hundred pounds. The doctor's voice faintly drifts into the background. I stare past the doctor while he continues to explain what will happen next. I blankly look at Greyson's awkward sleeping position on the hospital waiting-room chairs. Chow Mein. The doctor says something about more tests and monitoring damage to the organs, and I recall Dennis' plate of Chow Mein noodles. While we were out to dinner this past Sunday evening, Dennis complained of numbness in his left arm. He kept moving it around to relieve the tingling feeling. I didn't think anything of it because of his line of work. I thought maybe he'd strained a muscle using his nail gun. If only it were that simple. Two days later, he is hospitalized.

I finally call my mother the next morning around 6:00 a.m. She is beside herself that we went through such an ordeal without calling her to be with us. Within a few hours, my parents, two close family friends, and my best girlfriends are at our house, cooking food, bringing groceries, washing the dishes, minding Greyson and Mckenna, sitting for reassurance, and asking what more I need. Although there is love and support around me, I am numb with fear. I don't know what I need or what to do, other than sit at his hospital bed and worry about him, about us.

Almost one week later, Dennis' blood pressure is stable and his vision intact. The doctor says it will take four to six months for him to recuperate and regain strength. I relay the update to everyone. A few days after the hospitalization, when my friends have gone and the kids are asleep, Matt and I sit at the dining-room table while my mother cleans the kitchen. There is an unsettling quietude hovering around each of us. Matt looks at the empty coffee cup in his hands without interest in coffee. I have an idea of what is on his mind because it is also on my mind. Looking at the empty cup, he carefully asks, "What's your financial situation?" He wants to know, but, then again, he doesn't. He wants me to say that we were fine, that there is no need to worry about the mortgage, but something about the way he asks suggests that he already knows that is not what I am going to say. "What financial situation?" I thought. There isn't much about our finances that can be considered a "situation." Dennis is our primary source of income, period. He was in the middle of a painting job the workers can finish without him. When they finish, I will have to collect the final payment from the homeowner to pay the workers and us. Dennis was also at the beginning stage of a kitchen remodel and we already deposited the down payment check. We will have to return the deposit if we can't work out an agreement with the homeowners. The unemployment extension I received from being laid off from teaching ended months ago, along with COBRA. The little money we have in the bank and the money from the painting job can cover the mortgage for maybe two months. We will need help, and by the look on my step-father's face, I know my parents can only do so much. Every detail of our life is breaking. I get up from the table and walk into the kids' bedroom. The peaceful rhythm of their inhales and exhales provide momentary relief. "'With the loss of Dennis' income and the lack of emergency funds to sustain us…'" I don't want my thoughts to go any further. I quietly walk over to the nightstand and reach for the lamp. With one turn of the switch, the light on our way forward has gone out.

Five months have passed since Dennis was released from the hospital. Although his health is improving, he isn't ready to take on strenuous work projects. Not only does he have to adjust to physical limitations, but also to the emotional toll of worrying about his health and work. We are both worried about work, money, and health. It doesn't take long for the mental strain to take a toll on our relationship. There is an overwhelming sense of unease in not knowing what will come next, if Dennis really is okay, and who will watch Mckenna if I return to work. The rapid decline of any semblance of security over the past few months leaves both of us on edge, angry at the slightest verbal misstep, but, even more, afraid.

Before Dennis, the kids, and house, I was excited about the opportunities life presented: that I would be professionally accomplished, with choices and perpetual happiness. I entered the workforce as an independent woman, and barely existed in the present moment because I was so excited about my future. After Dennis, the kids and the house, I was still happy, until five months ago when things changed. Now, the future I was so excited about entails unanticipated maternal desires and being late on the mortgage for my childhood home, which Dennis worked so hard to renovate. Last week was horrible. Dennis and I had an explosive argument. We went too far with insults, blame, and accusations. It was terrible to see I could participate in such volatile anger. After the argument, I sat up for most of the night thinking about the anger we displayed and how much Greyson and Mckenna may have heard, even though they were in bed. Only deep rage will speak, cast blame, yell, and break things in the manner in which we did. The kids don't have to hear us argue. They know something is going on, even though we try to hide it. They are extremely perceptive. They sense tension in our body language, facial expressions, and the tone in which we sometimes speak to each other. Dennis is angry that I'm still home with Mckenna and I'm angry he cannot support us. This situation has not only brought primal fears out into the open, but is also shedding light on the depths of our emotional wounds. I'm scared and I know he is too. I love him, and I know he loves me, but right now, neither of us feels loved by the other. We are now two months behind on the mortgage.

I will have to ask my parents for help to cover at least one month's mortgage payment. I really do not want to ask for help because asking for help requires a conversation. The monthly mortgage statement is mailed to our house, so they are unaware we have fallen behind. In a desperate attempt to ask them for as little money as possible, Dennis and I pawn our wedding rings, a few pieces of jewelry and some of his tools. It is surreal to walk into a pawn shop with a Movado watch given to me by my mother. Of course, we don't get much, but it is something to put towards the mortgage. Worrying about the mortgage falling further behind, calling the loan servicer, and sending in what we have for payments pushes me to the limit. I am now applying for work. In September of 2006, after less than two months of looking, I am hired and return to work.

Since I've been a stay-at-home mom for three years, my hourly pay is shockingly reduced. As a teacher, my final hourly rate was close to twenty-five dollars, and I supported myself with this income. The position I've accepted at USC, however, pays fourteen dollars per hour. With a monthly salary of $2,250 before taxes, yes, this will fully cover the mortgage, late fees, and penalties, if we don't need to eat; if we don't put gas in the cars, pay for childcare, pay the car note, car insurance, utilities and telephone bills, and the co-pay for medical prescriptions. We will still have to pick and choose what and when to pay. Nonetheless, I say okay to the hourly rate and don't dare jeopardize anything by asking to negotiate for more. The bills are now so out of control that paying them seems like a fantasy from a previous life.

With me working, household chores are building up along with the pile of bills on the desk. I simply refuse to do everything I did as a stay-at-home mom and work. It is too much to go to work, take care of the kids, cook and clean because I am too exhausted. In fact, I am abnormally exhausted. My mind is overly occupied with thoughts, questions, worries, fears, and even hope; hope for anything better than this. I have passed many days feeling cheated, like a victim, like I'm drowning. Why are we experiencing this? What do we need to learn that warrants this? It seems like our life is at a standstill, like we're waiting for a miracle. But the miracle isn't showing up, or at least not the miracle I have I mind. Things are getting worse because we cannot get current on the bills. And, to make matters worse, every single day there is a voice, a feeling, an idea, something within me that says, "Write." *Every single day.* And every single day, my mental response is, "But I'm not that good of a writer. I don't know what to write about. I don't have any money or resources to spend time on writing." I'm not sure what this feeling is about, or where it stems from, but it is persistent. I have kept a journal since I was in fourth grade, and I still have every single one of them. I have always enjoyed writing and have long told myself I will one day write a book, but how can I write now? My mind is too distracted. I have too many things to worry about.

Since I started working, Dennis is more involved with the kids. He takes Greyson to Cub Scouts meetings, takes him to school, cooks breakfast, and helps with lunch preparation. He's experiencing the effort required to take care of children, manage a household, and work, and he doesn't seem to mind. Household cleaning chores are another matter. When I was home, the house was clean all the time. Now it's a disaster. When I come home from work, I look the other way and ignore the dirty dishes, just like he does. Last month we set a record. I refused to clean the kitchen and so did he. He says he doesn't like to wash dishes. Oh really? The dirty dishes sat in the kitchen sink for three weeks! I finally gave in when my friend said she was coming over.

Seeing that I've been so tired and lethargic, and now that we have medical coverage again, Dennis insists that I go to the doctor. We have our moments of dipping in and out of arguments, having off-and-on power struggles over who is doing the most, and sometimes finding solace in each other late at night when the kids are asleep. When I go to the doctor and tell her how tired I feel, she insists I take a pregnancy test. I assume she's joking, until she rolls the ultrasound machine into the exam room. Why do I need a pregnancy test if I'm still having a period? She puts the gel onto my lower belly and slowly moves the wand around. "What the…?!!" I gasp. The black-and-white image on the monitor displays a leg, an arm, and something that resembles a head! I am almost four months pregnant and didn't know it! Apparently, it wasn't a period. It was spotting. And the miracle I didn't have in mind is due in six months. Although this pregnancy is not miraculous by a standard definition, miracles come in many forms. Whether it is the baby, the internal prompt to write, or finding a new way of being, there is something undiscovered within me wanting to come into the world. Like the slow development of the baby, for me to move into new ways of thinking and perceiving life, the change I will have to undergo will also require gestation. I will have to undergo two birthing events—one for the baby and one for me—to understand that the origin of everything I need is within me. Our third child, Gavin, is born in April of 2007.

When my three-month maternity leave ends in July of 2007, it isn't an option to enroll Gavin at the same facility as Mckenna. The monthly rate for infants is $1,200! Mckenna has one more year in preschool. She can feed herself, is potty-trained, and it still costs $700 a month. Greyson is now in second grade, and is supervised on the playground after school until Dennis picks him up. I return to work on a part-time basis, but we have to get creative on how we will manage a childcare situation that allows me to continue to breastfeed without going deeper into debt. I explain all of this to the Project Manager, my immediate supervisor, and request to bring the baby to work with me two days a week. My mother agrees to watch the baby on Mondays, which leaves Wednesdays and Fridays for me to navigate with him at work. The Project Manager discusses the situation with the two primary Project Investigators. Both women agree to my request.

During my work hours, I work diligently while Gavin sleeps, and do not waste any time socializing. I take him to meetings, carry him in Greyson's Baby Bjorn when I deliver paperwork, and walk around outside with him in the stroller, so he will drift off to sleep after my lunch break. Having a baby at work is inconvenient, but I make it work for a little over a year with my annual performance review resulting in "Exceeds Expectations" across the majority of categories.

Things are moving along, although not necessarily in the best way. The kids, Dennis, and I trek through the daily routine of domestic and professional responsibilities while the country surreptitiously moves deeper into economic crisis. Then, during the worst of the economic downturn in 2009, funding for our research project is frozen and the grant not renewed. I am laid off from work.

With the layoff, I have the option to withdraw the full amount of funds from my retirement account, or leave it as is. With close to three years working on the project, I accrued roughly $6,000 in that account. With Dennis' secondary signature of approval, I make the withdrawal. We put the money towards our living expenses and some towards the mortgage, but we are still behind on the mortgage. By now, my parents are receiving telephone calls from the loan servicer, and I am trying to avoid going over to their house. That is impossible because my mother wants to spend time with the kids. I resort to trying to drop the kids off when I hope Matt isn't home. Sometimes it works, sometimes it doesn't. One Saturday night, he is home. When I walk into the house, I can feel the tension before I turn the corner to greet him in his dining room chair. A bill from the loan servicer lies on the table in front of him. "We're going to lose that house," he says. "And we might lose this house! This is going to ruin us. I cannot believe you let this happen! This is not how we raised you. We don't have $16,000 to give these people!" At that moment, I should have said, "I'm sorry." I should have told him how sorry I am that Dennis and I did not keep our end of the agreement, and that I am so sorry our choices affected them this way. But that's not what I do. I stand in silence whirling in embarrassment, anger, fear, and disdain for everything, and instead of apologizing, I try to defend myself. Maybe I did wait too long to return to work. Maybe I should not have been home with Mckenna in the first place. Maybe I should have asked for more money when I was hired at USC. No matter how much we put towards the mortgage, we cannot catch up and stay up. My stepfather and I, the two most defensive individuals in the family, are primed for an argument over the house on Forty-first, and argue we do. I don't have any reason or right to defend the fact that the house they refinanced for us is in pre-foreclosure, but I do. Despite my defensive position, I feel terrible. I feel so alone. I am sorry for everything, and I cry on the drive home.

Since we moved into the house, the mortgage has been sold to two different loan servicers. Each time the loan is bundled and sold, vital information regarding our payment history is "lost," and always to the advantage of the lenders. We lived through a four-year cycle of sending in money orders for the mortgage, missing monthly payments, avoiding creditor phone calls, having the water and power shut off and restored, borrowing money from my closest friends, regretting borrowing money from my closest friends, hoping the neighbors won't notice random strangers standing in the middle of the street photographing the house, and watching property investors in nice cars periodically stop in front of our house to get a good look. The prolonged loss of a home takes a staggering toll on physical and emotional health, because we create emotional meaning tied to where we live. A home is normally a place of refuge and sanctuary; it's where you find safety and comfort, and create lasting memories with people you love. But when you're dealing with foreclosure, the house no longer feels safe. It's no longer comfortable. It becomes a living reminder of instability. You can no longer do simple acts with simplicity. Every act–washing the dishes, folding laundry, cooking dinner, walking outside (only to see someone photographing the house)–is contaminated with a perpetual fear of loss.

One afternoon, during another prolonged session of feeling sorry for myself, I lie on the sofa aimlessly flipping through the channels. I come across Elizabeth Gilbert, speaking about her book *Eat, Pray, Love* on Oprah. I'm not in the mood to hear yet another story of how wonderful life is coming from someone so far removed from my life. As I listen, I begin to feel simultaneously excited to read the book, yet sad. After a few minutes, I realize I am no longer listening to a word she's saying, as if the television is on mute. I notice the radiance in this woman's eyes; her spirit is beaming out from her eyes and piercing the television screen! How can it be that I am sitting thousands of miles away, yet I know this woman is completely filled with love and inner peace? This sends a disturbing wake-up call through my system. I try to recall a moment, any moment in recent times, when my eyes shone with joy of this magnitude. The truth is that there isn't a recent memory when I display such happiness, because I am not happy. I am unrecognizable to myself; wandering aimlessly, feeling overwhelmed with work, the financial situation, the strain on my marriage, and the immense shock of it all. I feel lethargically uninspired, angry, and simply put-off with the entire deal. My mind is filled with noise, and I am changing as a result of the crisis. I let it become a part of me. It permeates every aspect of my day, interactions, and thoughts. Being faced with the issue of homelessness, not knowing where we will sleep, having so few options, thinking about our family being split apart, not knowing if we will qualify to rent an apartment, is taking a profound emotional toll on me, and on us. It takes vast amounts of effort to hold myself together, to not be depressed, and to quell complaints of victimization. When I visit family and friends, it is difficult to relax. I notice the abundance of food, household supplies, and unnecessary stuff lying around. I think, "Look at all this stuff! Look at what they can afford to buy. They are relaxed because they have money. They are not worried about losing their house." The only person who truly knows how little money we have is my good friend, a certified tax preparer, who files our taxes. I can only talk about crisis so much, and then I stop. In my world, the crisis is all there is, but in the lives of friends and family who are doing fine, they can only do and say so much.

With the weight of all of this on my mind, I want desperately to feel relief, to feel inspired. So, I start saying aloud, "I just want to be inspired," over and over again. Without realizing what is happening, by voicing aloud that I want to feel inspired, I proclaim I am finally ready to receive help. A few days later, after service at my mother's spiritual center, my mother stops by our house. I have attended service with her a few times. The reverend speaks of quieting the mind, turning within through meditation and personal transformation, things I have not ever heard in a church service. I'm not sure how these recommendations can help with our current situation, but nevertheless, I'm curious. When my mother stops by late Sunday morning, she has two books she's bought for me. She occasionally stops by on Sundays after church to visit with the kids and comes bearing gifts. Despite everything, she is absolute with unconditional love. She doesn't bring up the argument with Matt or the mortgage. She hands me the two books, one of which is the initiator of a spiritual watershed moment. "I bought these for you." *The Power of Intention*, by Dr. Wayne Dyer, boldly catches my attention.

Trusting my mother's judgment, over the course of the next few days I read *The Power of Intention*. Change, intention, perception, thoughts become things, silence, meditation, energy, transformation, and clarity are not foreign to me, but then again, they are. I have not heard these words explained in a way I can relate to and apply to challenges in my life. The book is by no means the answer to my problems, but it is another unexpected miracle. It sparks curiosity. I want to know more about how perception influences our experience of life, how we attract things, situations and people into our lives that reflect our level of consciousness. I want to know more about consciousness, what it is, and the role it plays in my life. I want to know more about spirituality, how I can once again feel connected to life and have faith. And I want to know how to begin on my own because I cannot afford a therapist. The book is the beginning of inspiration—exactly what I need. I finish the book within a few days, and listen to the library audiobook three times over the next few weeks. Asking for inspiration and then starting to receive it opened me up to a new way of thinking, a new way of perceiving life, and a new approach to living it. I am ready to acknowledge I have orchestrated a mess. I am ready to understand which intentions brought me to the chaos that now encompasses every aspect of my life. From the book, I begin to understand the following:

- If you change the way you look at things, the things you look at will change.

- Before any action is taken, decide what it is you really want, and set the intention.

- Be reflective and stop all judgment of yourself and others.

- Meditate consistently to reconnect with yourself.

- Be appreciative. Showing gratitude begins the internal shift that allows you to see love and connection to all things.

Considering these ideas, I realize I haven't been fully honest with myself, or Dennis, in my decision to stay at home. Of course I wanted to be there for Greyson and Mckenna, but on a deeper level I also wanted to force Dennis to take care of me so I would feel loved. When I pushed so hard for something we couldn't afford, I didn't realize there was a subconscious emotional need underlying my decision—that a deeply wounded part of myself played a part in guiding the decision. It is very easy to blame all the problems I experienced on Dennis' illness, my family, and my situation—all things outside of me. It is, however, extremely difficult to accept that I need to take a deeply thorough look at myself and my role in creating the ugliness.

I quietly begin to devote myself to emotional healing. I read more books related to spiritual growth, and notice a common theme throughout the books: the benefits of quieting the mind through meditation and prayer. If this many authors are saying the exact same thing, it must have merit.

When I first begin to meditate, I am desperate for someone, something, anything to save me from my problems. I actually remember thinking, "Maybe if I meditate for a few weeks, all of my problems will just go away." Despite the initial difficulty of the mental seesaw between tiny gaps of stillness and stressful thoughts, I continue to meditate. It seems everything that bothers me during the day wants my attention during meditation. I experience brief moments of feeling quiet, safe, and at ease, then I think of something that bothers me. A rotation of duality plays out in my mind: calm/fear, ease/disease, anger/peace. Every emotion I feel, but do not completely express, comes up for review. I don't know what this duality means, or if I'm "doing it right;" nevertheless I continue. Each night, it becomes a little easier. While simultaneously experiencing brief moments of silence, I also observe the negative patterns in my beliefs which rise up for review. The brief moments of stillness allow space to become aware of the dominant thoughts and beliefs I hold, and to see unhealthy patterns in my thoughts. I continue to meditate late at night, after the kids and Dennis are asleep. I do this for months alongside the impending arrival of the foreclosure. Meditation helps me to feel more relaxed, but it is momentary. I am under a lot of stress, we are under a lot of stress, and meditation consistently provides momentary relief to cope with the situation.

Then, one day, amidst intermittent calm throughout the day, I pull into the driveway after picking the kids up from school and notice something on the front door. There are two white pieces of paper taped to the front door, visible to everyone. We are beyond the period to reinstate the loan and stop the foreclosure process. It is the Notice of Foreclosure Trustee Sale. The house will be sold in thirty days. I am shaken with fear and the thought of having to tell Dennis, and my parents, it is officially over. There are no more delays, no more holding it off, requests for more time. It is done. The date of the sale is set. Two days later, at 7:20 a.m., as I back out of the driveway to take the kids to school, a man runs up to the car, hastily knocks on the car window and ask, "Do you live here?" I roll the window down just enough to hear him clearly. "Yes." He says, "Great. These are for you. You've been served," and slides the papers through the car window opening. When I return from dropping the kids off, a different man stands in our front yard pounding a "For Sale" sign down into the grass. When he finishes, the sign is tall and white, visible as soon as you make the turn onto the block. In less than thirty days, we have to figure out what to do with our furniture and the new appliances, and where we will go. One month earlier, my parents contacted a realtor to sell the house. For two weekends we had to leave so the realtor could hold "Open House." There was one offer made on the house, but we are not sure why the bank did not accept the offer.

In July 2010, the day of the sale, the day we tried to delay and prevent for four years has arrived. That morning, there are no neighbors outside to say goodbye to and no visit from a bank official. It is depressingly anti-climactic in a way I never imagined. With no warning, or prior notice in the mail, the power shuts off at 8:00 a.m. In the eerily quiet and empty house, Dennis and I do a final walk-through. We had watched news reports of disgruntled foreclosed homeowners who destroyed the house before moving out; a "screw you" to the bank. We don't break anything. There was too much love put into the house to destroy anything. The experience has destroyed enough. After a few minutes of silence, Dennis asks, "Are you ready to go?" I'm not, but I answer, "Yes." Quietly and uneventfully, with no sign of the mental and emotional trauma we went through, we walk out of the house for the last time. He starts the truck engine and slowly pulls forward out of the driveway. It is over. We drive to the end of the block to the stop sign, as we have done many times before, as if nothing is different. But everything is different. We are different. And we have no idea what comes next.

I stay at my parents' house with the kids, without Dennis. He can't bear to face my parents. I can't bear to face my parents, but there is nowhere else to go. Dennis goes to stay with a cousin, and I begin to look for an apartment.

Because we made so little money, we received a few thousand dollars in our tax refund. Hopefully, it will be enough for an apartment rental deposit and to live on for a few months. We are both anxious that we won't pass a credit check to rent an apartment, on top of me being out of work and the construction industry still reeling from the downturn. In addition to looking for an apartment, now is a good time to do something about the voice, the feeling, the idea that says, "Write." I stumble upon Examiner.com, which is hiring writers. I apply, and, after submitting three writing samples, I am brought on to write as the National Spirituality Examiner. When I find the apartment I want to apply for, which happens to be a three-minute drive from the spiritual center I attend with my mother, I list my employment as a writer with a monthly income of $1,000. Payment for writing is based on page views. Surely I can generate enough views to make $1,000.

When I meet the landlord and disclose that we have issues on our credit report, with gentle and surprising softness in her voice, she says, "When I was down, somebody helped me. Everyone deserves a second chance." Two weeks after losing the house to foreclosure, we sign the lease and move into our new apartment.

By Christmas, we are fully settled in. I now attend service at the spiritual center weekly with the kids. Greyson and Mckenna attend the same elementary school, and Gavin attends preschool three days a week, while Dennis and I try to create a stable routine despite the finances. I write articles for Examiner on the days Gavin attends preschool. However, the disappointing reality is that the writing income I naively anticipated I could create within a matter of months will take longer than I thought. Discouragement quietly settles in underneath the weight of living expenses, bills, and five mouths to feed...including my own.

I have now been meditating and reading for close to a year. A consistent theme in many of the books is that, in order to receive help, you have to ask for help, as I did when I said aloud, "I just want to be inspired," and my mother stopped by with the books. Writing isn't working out in the way I've hoped it would, and what is left of our tax refund is almost gone. During one morning meditation, after a sustained period of silence and prayer, it occurs to me that I can ask for guidance to come into my awareness. The first time nothing happens. Then, around the third or fourth time, I notice words floating in from the left side of my awareness. It isn't a voice, or anything I can identify as something outside of myself. They are words, with an extremely loving presence, which float in like a subtle breeze. At first, I think, "I must be making this up. It must be my imagination." As I continue to listen, over more meditation sessions, I realize the words are not words, phrases, or sentence structures I use. Simply put, I don't talk like this; therefore, it can't be from something I've made up or imagined, yet I feel a connection. So I continue to listen and feel for the loving presence of the words, which I now refer to as guidance. However, as soon as the meditation is over, I forget what came up. I decide to bring a large pad and pen to my meditation sessions because I want to remember everything. It is too important to miss anything. I've also read about the importance of surrounding myself with love and light when asking for guidance, so I add the following words to signify I am ready to listen and be protected:

"I call upon my Higher Self to join me in my meditation. During this meditation, I ask that you protect me from any and all vibrations, energies, frequencies, and communications in all directions of time, past, present and future, that are not of love, light, and the highest good. Please let this communication be clear. Let the answers be communicated to me in a way that is easy for me to understand. Please let me feel your loving energy when you are ready to begin. I thank you in advance for your presence."

At the time, I didn't have the awareness to perceive possibility in crisis, or know that, years later, I would be grateful for the personal and spiritual growth which resulted from the loss of the house. The dismantling of life as I knew it had to occur so I could put myself back together, not in fragments, but in wholeness. Whether I was aware of it or not, the loss of the house on Forty-first was the impetus from which I began to choose something new. It was the beginning of my spiritual journey before I even realized what it was. But such is the nature of a gift—it is given freely, accepted willingly, and arrives when it is least expected.

CHAPTER TWO

NOTICE TO QUIT

Meditation is not something that entered my life with ease. There were many times when I thought I couldn't meditate, and that quieting the mind is not a viable way to deal with problems. I had so much on my mind, so much to worry about, and so much to figure out. I thought, "Who has time to meditate? I surely don't. I have worrying to do."

Pressing financial concerns arrive with each overdue bill in the mail. Every day, when I hear the mailman arrive and drop more envelopes into our mailbox, I think, "What now?" Retrieving the mail has become a slow walk of misery. Good news is rarely delivered via the mail. These days we only receive stern requests printed in large red letters. Each time I look at the accumulated mail on the corner of my desk, it seems irresponsible and negligent to *not* worry.

One morning, right around the time the mail is usually delivered, the doorbell rings. It startles me. I'm not expecting anyone. I get up from the dining-room table and walk to the front door. Before I look through the peephole, a male voice loudly announces, "Gas company!" My heart drops! Good news is rarely delivered by anyone outside your front door announcing, "Gas company!" If I pretend to not be at home, the gas will surely be shut off. But if I open the door, I'll have to give payment. My checking account balance is -$12.32. I hesitantly unlock the door, open it, and say, "Yes?" with phony cluelessness, as if I don't know what he wants. In a surprisingly kind and non-confrontational manner, the Gas Company employee says, "Good morning, ma'am. I'm here to collect payment for past due gas service. You have a past due amount of $120.94 that needs to be paid today in order to maintain gas service. You can pay by cash, check, debit, or credit card." He kindly gives the payment options as if it matters. I don't have $120 cash, nor do I have credit cards with available funds. The debit transaction will, of course, be declined. I do, however, have plenty of blank checks. My only option is to write a check for the past due amount and hope Dennis makes a deposit into my account before the check is deposited for clearance. "I can write a check." "Okay," he says nonchalantly, "but just so you know, if you write a check that doesn't clear, you won't be able to pay by check for gas service for a period of twelve months." "Okay," I say, trying to hide my discomfort. I ask him to wait a moment while I walk to the bedroom to get my checkbook out of my purse. With my checkbook and pen in hand, I walk back to the dining-room table and begin to write the check for the past due amount. As I write the words *one-hundred-twenty-dollars* on the second line of the check, my hands nervously tremble. The temperature in the dining room seems to rise with every letter and number I write on the face of the check. I carefully tear the check from the checkbook, walk back to the front door, and hand the check to him. He does whatever gas company employees do on their machines when they stand at your door while you maintain an awkward silence. "Oh my Gosh!" I stare at his machine. "Please, please, please don't let that be an instant check scanner!" I stand motionless, hoping the worst is not about to happen. Then he hands me the payment receipt, smiles, and says, "Thank you. Have a good day." It is done. The kids can take a hot shower before going to bed, I can continue to use the stove to cook, and Dennis will have to be told that he has to cover the $120.94 check and the negative balance of $12.32. I close the front door, walk over to the couch, and fall back in a defeated slump. "What am I going to do? What are we going to do? How long can this go on?"

A few hours later, as I drive to pick up the kids after school, I squeeze the steering wheel, and it is hard to steady my breath. My heart races as I gasp for air with short, quick breaths. I have not had an anxiety attack in my life, but on this day, discouraging and repetitive thoughts race through my mind like a runaway train. With cunning determination and unprecedented speed, my thoughts have a mind of their own. They scream, "I'm going to die! I can't take this anymore! We're going to have to move in with my parents! I don't want to live with my parents. Will the check clear? Who is going to take in a family of five? Can he deposit the money in time? Or realistically a family of four? I'm so embarrassed! I'm so ashamed! I hate my life! I'm so tired of this!" Thoughts flow one after the other in a continuous loop until, for a moment, I forget I'm driving. When my attention returns to the present moment, I pull the car over and park on a residential street a few blocks away from Mckenna and Gavin's elementary school. I turn off the engine and sit inside the car in silence. I watch the cars passing by on the street and the crossing guard at the stop sign. Most of the cars are shiny, new models with drivers who appear happy, with no concerns of past due gas payments and eviction. For everyone else, it is a beautiful sunny afternoon. "Everybody is doing better than Dennis and me. Everybody. How can there be so much money in this world and we don't have any of it?" I let my head fall back onto the headrest and begin to cry. Tears of disappointment for all I hoped to become roll down my cheeks until I hear the end-of-school bell ring in the distance. I sit up, pull down the vanity mirror, and look at my face. This is never the life I intended to live. Years ago, when I sat in my dorm room at Cal and reveled in the joy of my future prospects, and the ways in which I would change the world to make a difference, I never imagined destitution and hardship as possible outcomes in my life. I never imagined this moment, that I would sit here, parked outside my children's school, wiping away tears of sadness and desperation.

I get out of the car and walk onto the school campus, toward the preschool playground. I don't make eye contact with anyone, and take calculated steps to avoid potential conversations. I'm not up for a discussion about tomorrow's PTA meeting, classroom supplies, or which parent volunteer has dropped the ball. I just want to pick up the kids and get back to feeling sorry for myself. I stop at the gated entrance to the preschool playground and look around the yard for Gavin. There he is, riding one of those yellow Lakeshore trikes as fast as he can. He sees me standing at the gate, and, like always, he smiles in a way that pulls me out of time. In the midst of feverish pedaling, he lets go of one of the trike handles and waves as he yells across the yard, "Hi mommy!" The joy in his voice flows with unobstructed delight. I sit down on the bench to watch him play while I wait for Mckenna. The sight of Gavin romping around the yard, and the other children playing, reminds me of aspects of myself I have lost.

Light emanating from the children's tiny little faces softens the tightness that dominates mine. Running around the yard, their eyes glisten with excitement, lightness, and the enthusiasm of unhindered possibility. The chatter of their voices, and sounds of joyful giggles, are remnants of all I remember to be hopeful and anchored in love. Unlike me, they are boundless. They play unencumbered by bad decisions and the lingering tension of unknown outcomes. They are free in a way I long to recapture and once again hold in my heart.

Mckenna walks through the gate into the preschool yard and sits down on the bench beside me. I give her a kiss on the cheek and stand up. Gavin sees Mckenna and knows his playtime is over. He jumps off the trike, skips over the hopscotch, runs underneath the slide, and jumps up to hit the monkey bars one last time before landing in front of me and wrapping his arms around my waist. I smile and hold onto the comfort of his loving affection. I hold onto him, and feel my heart. Despite everything, it is still beating.

When we return to the car, I unlock the doors and walk to the passenger side to place their backpacks on the front seat. Mckenna takes off her backpack and drops it on top of *The Untethered Soul*, a book I'm reading that lies on the front seat. I look at the book as the backpack covers it. "What is the point? Why do I continue to waste my time reading all these books if I don't take the recommendations to heart? At some point I have to decide if I really believe in this stuff or not."

We get into the car and drive five minutes to the middle school to pick up Greyson. When we pull up to the middle school, Greyson is standing out front, waiting with two of his friends. Of all the things I could have done differently, having these children is not one of them. Embodying a sacred essence that is good, whole, and complete, unknowingly, their presence pulls at love within me. With each passing day, they inspire me to begin again.

I put the car in drive and push down on the accelerator. Mckenna and Gavin sit in the back seat, arguing over who will eat the leftover chips from Gavin's lunchbox. Greyson quietly looks out the window while Marley's words drift throughout the car "...*don't worry about a thing, 'cause every little thing gonna be alright...*"

As soon as we get home, I get the kids settled with an after-school snack and immediately go into our bedroom to meditate. I know from previous experience that I will feel calmer after meditation.

I close the door behind me and lock it. Once their after-school snack is finished, questions, comments, and requests inevitably begin. I want to ensure that I have at least twenty minutes without interruption. I draw the blinds, then grab a pillow to situate behind my back. I sit down on my favorite spot on the bed with my back against the headboard. I take one pillow and place it behind my lower back for support. When I meditate, my back gets tired. The muscle strain gets uncomfortable and distracts my focus. The next thing I know I'm distracted, and thinking about my back instead of nothing. Maybe, for some, the assistance of the pillow is considered a cheat, but for now, my cheat helps me make progress.

To begin, I sit with my legs crossed and my arms resting on my thighs, with both palms open and facing upward. With palms open, my chest and back straight, I am receptive and ready to welcome what will come and what needs to come. Sitting in this position reiterates to my mind, body and heart that I want to know something more than what my outward experiences have shown; that I am ready and willing to connect to the wisdom, stillness and love of a Higher Intelligence within myself. I glance at the clock, then let my eyes close to draw my attention inward, away from all things unimportant. I withdraw into the darkness beneath my eyes and hear the rhythmic beat of my heart. With every heartbeat, I recognize the flow of life moving within me and I am moved to give thanks. I begin with a prayer of gratitude. Despite unwanted circumstances, I give thanks for this moment of knowing I am well and my family is well; for the food we will later eat, and for this place we still call home. The words fade off into the distance. I hold my focus on the air flowing in and flowing out. Like my heartbeat, I find rhythm in my breath. This is where I stay, letting all things unimportant fade away until I reach inward soundlessness. A few moments pass, and there is a quick resurgence of uninvited thoughts. "The check might not clear. He's going to be upset. What are the kids doing? Why can't I win a shopping spree at Costco?" Thoughts are relentless; always trying to make themselves heard, hold a place in my mind and assert their problem-reinforcing agenda. Right now, I don't want to be pulled back into the misery of things, so I simply notice their presence. The thoughts are there without me "taking the bait" to follow them up. This was the problem earlier today, during my downward spiral into fearful and negative thoughts. In a state of fear and hopelessness, I believed the fear-mongering thoughts. Once these type of thoughts begin, it's best not to follow them up. If you don't let the thoughts drift away, they create momentum to drag you where they want you to go. This precisely is one of the benefits of meditation. You begin to understand that thoughts are just thoughts, and you don't have to believe everything you think. You can let the thoughts pass through your awareness without attaching to them. This, however, is not something that can be done instantly. It takes practice and dedication in meditation to get better at observing thoughts, instead of constantly being pulled around by them, like I was today.

Within a few moments of coming back to the lightness of my breath, the thoughts fade into soundlessness, as do I.

Once my mind is still for a period of time, I allow the thoughts I choose to re-enter my mind as I prepare to invite guidance. I think of the professional vision I hold for my life. My vision encompasses a continued intention to be a writer who provides meaningful, high-vibrational information which creates a bridge for personal growth. Embedded within this vision for my professional life is also the intention to be able to support myself, and my family, through creative pursuits. I would like nothing more than to be in the financial position to consistently pay all of my personal bills, and living expenses, in full and on time every single month without interruption. As a paid professional, it is also my intention to establish an emergency fund to avoid situations like this one. I want to be a living demonstration to my children of what it looks like to speak and act from a place of personal authenticity, creative integrity, financial modesty, and responsibility. Because we have on many occasions been on the receiving end of generosity and compassion, I want to pay it forward by making monetary donations to philanthropic organizations that encourage mindful living, feminine empowerment, and a conscious business model. Within this scope, I would also love to work on collaborative projects with people who are sincere, authentic individuals of integrity who also hold a vision of making meaningful and innovative contributions to the world. On a personal level, my vision for deeper personal development is to gain clarity to understand what produced the original condition of lack in my mind. What did I have to believe in order to restrict my ability to manifest meaningful work? And what did I have to believe in order to create such prolonged financial hardship?

With the aforementioned vision and questions hovering in my awareness, I hold my attention within and say the following:

"I call upon my Higher Self to join me in my meditation. During this meditation, I ask that you protect me from any and all vibrations, energies, frequencies, and communications in all directions of time, past, present, and future, that are not of love, light, and the highest good. Please let this communication be clear. Let the answers be communicated to me in a way that is easy for me to understand. Please let me feel your loving energy when you are ready to begin. I thank you in advance for your presence."

I sit quietly, wait, and then ask, "For the questions and vision I now hold in my awareness, what vital information do you have for me today?"

After having posed my questions in the form of thinking about the questions, I also hold in my awareness the concerns that I'd like to have addressed during meditation. I sit quietly and wait for internal guidance that is rooted in clarity, and flows in the form of words to me. In this instance, it would appear as though I am "talking to myself." However, having done this before, as well as using discernment, I know the guidance that comes to me does not represent my voice, my words, or my thoughts on a conscious level. The guidance reveals itself in the form of words that represent a soft, loving, and consistent connection to a higher internal intelligence that is devoid of the anxiety, doubt, and worry which is normally housed in my verbal expressions. This internal Higher Intelligence does not ever direct or tell me what to do. The guidance addresses my questions and concerns in a manner that presents overarching information that speaks to the big picture of what is taking place. It offers options and suggestions in a routinely loving manner. As much as I want to be told what to do, to whom I should direct a call or email, or which is the most immediate course of relief for my financial concerns, the guidance does not provide that type of response. The response is always a consistent reassurance of wellness, that I am loved, that we are loved, and that I and we are never alone. In this sense, it is loving encouragement. No matter what comes through during meditation, it is always my decision, my discernment, and my free will, what I decide to do with the guidance that is provided.

That afternoon, as I sit on the bed, this is the guidance that comes through:

Let the vision reveal itself. *By holding yourself back and not sharing your gifts with the world, you have already tried to minimize your need for a life of service. You have repeatedly told yourself, "I can live with this, or I can live that. I can live without having the life I really want." Deep within yourself you know mediocrity is a slow death because you've tried it. You tried to remain in situations (professional and personal) that on a soul level you knew were no longer beneficial, and it didn't work. Be fully who you are with no restrictions and no excuses. This life you have is for you to be who you are meant to be. You can feel who you are meant to be, which is why anything less is so unsettling. With the inner urge you feel to move toward creative expression, you are being called to be of service and share yourself. You are being called to show who you are, to express your gifts, and to live this every moment of every day. No exceptions. What has been said is direct, but know there is only love.*

Hold the vision. *You must hold the vision of what you would like to see manifest in your life and in this world. You must hold in your awareness what you would like to see manifest until it becomes a reality. Hold clear visions of your personal aspirations, goals, dreams, and ideas, while also holding the space for visions of peace, collaboration, and love for the collective whole. All mental, physical, emotional, and spiritual movement first begins as an idea. Then the idea becomes a feeling to inspire personal action. The action creates momentum in the belief that the idea you hold is possible, and then that idea ultimately emerges in your life, or as your life. We understand that you have questioned whether you can really create and have the life you want to live. Know that you can. But it first begins with the idea of what you want to create, how you nurture the idea through daily inspired action, or how you sabotage the idea through fear, doubt, and excessive worry.*

Your idea and vision for your life is nurtured when you believe in it; when you create a feeling of belief in your body that allows space for it to grow. You nurture the vision for your life when you act upon daily inspiration that tries to move you in the direction of your vision. You nurture the vision for your life when you know that the expression of it is also a manifestation of love. The love manifests in the form of service you give to the world by expressing your gifts. And you sabotage the vision for your life when your doubt is stronger than your belief. Every doubtful and fearful thought chips away at the foundation of the belief, and the possibility of the life and vision you hold becoming your daily reality.

You can have the life you dream of, but you have to believe you can. Step into belief and step towards what you want for your life. Step towards what you want to give to the world. Step into faith, because nothing less will do.

Trust the vision. *Life wants growth, change, an open heart, and a quiet mind. Life expresses itself abundantly when you remove your mental limitations. In order to remove mental limitations, do not believe everything you see and hear. There is so much more going on beneath the surface of outer appearances. You are to believe what your body tells you is true. As you trust yourself, you will come to know the soft, gentle feel of where truth resides within your body. You can use your self-trust to identify your soul center and use it to discern what is true. Your soul center is where you feel your connection to the presence of a Higher Intelligence. When information comes into your awareness, bring your attention to the place in your body where intuition is felt the strongest. Ask your question; for example, "Does this feel true for me? Does my body recognize truth in this information?" As you ask your question, pay attention to your body and feel the answer come into your awareness. You will become familiar with this feeling and will know the comfort that surrounds truth. Trust yourself. Be comfortable with truth and be comfortable in truth. There is only love and light.*

Surrender. *We feel that deeply lodged within you is a concern that you are doing something wrong. It is not a question of what you are "doing wrong." It is a matter of accepting where you are, letting it be what it is, and letting it pass. Stop holding onto it by giving so much of your attention to it and let it go. Let it be what it is meant to be and let it happen. Just let it all fall away. Let the worry fall away. There is no need to cling to the unknown from a place of fear. Instead, cling to the freeness of knowing that life is for you.*

You have to surrender over all that concerns you. You have lost control and are now being forced to recognize the opportunity that lies in surrender. Surrender does not mean to sit and do nothing, nor does surrender mean to give up or relinquish your power. Surrender means you relax into acceptance of where you are and what is happening around you. You let your body release the tension and angst of you trying to control the outcome of how you think things should be. It is letting go, and letting it be, so that whatever the situation or circumstance is trying to reveal to you can be shown to you. If your energy continues to remain tight, filled with worry and fear, you hold the situation and circumstance in your life. You don't need any tricks or resources to let go and surrender. You need faith, inspired thought, and then action upon these thoughts. Remember, when all is falling down around you, sometimes it's best to be still. Be still until it passes. We know you are worried about providing for yourself and your family, but you are not going to starve; nor are you going to die. You are being reborn.

Each step requires surrender of doubt and fear and all that has brought you to this point of letting go of everything that anchors you to despair. We know it is difficult to let go of ways that have "served" you in the past; the self-sabotaging ways that helped you to cope with all that is undesirable in your life. The time for coping has fallen away because the surrendering has begun as the candle has been lit. This is your time to leave all the ways of being that no longer serve you behind. This is your moment, the culmination of all you have learned, lived, wondered about ("Is this real, or am I crazy?"), to walk through the doorway of surrender and new beginnings. So let it be. There is only love.

At the close of my meditation, when the guidance is complete, I feel the energy withdraw and pull back. I place my hands in a prayerful *mudra* and say, "Thank you. This session is now over." I close the meditation session by declaring completion and gratitude. I remain seated within the silence for a few moments more and then open my eyes. Thirty minutes has passed. I like to begin with the intention of meditating for a minimum amount of time, but once I close my eyes and settle in, sometimes I want to pray a little longer, or I may want more silence. Either way, it's fine. As long as my intention is to honor the Higher Presence, guidance, and myself, I don't think there is a right or wrong way to meditate.

About a week later, with the gas service still on, I have a revelation. I get it now! This feels so liberating.

For the past few months, I have been praying and pleading for help to be saved from my problems, relieved of my worry and fears. I have, at the same time, looked toward hope, but did not see any manifestations of what I deemed to be a hopeful response. My hope is clouded by a perpetual residue of question and doubt. I meditate and believe the thoughts you think create your life, and I look for signs and guidance from the Universe. In this "looking," however, I continue to second-guess if this is real or if I'm living in a fantasy world. I have spent so much time wondering if I am projecting my desperate need for relief from my financial concerns, wanting change in my life, and my lack of patience onto the hope of trying to manifest the outcome; wondering if I am making things up, going off the "deep end" or living in denial. Being in so much doubt makes it difficult to accept what is being given to me, what is provided for me and my family. No wonder my life is so stagnant. It wasn't until we received the Notice to Quit for our apartment that I finally understood why it is necessary to give thanks in your darkest hour.

The evening of the fifteenth, I open the front door to walk to the mailbox. After getting the mail, I turn around to go back inside, and see an envelope taped to the front door. I know whatever is inside the envelope can't be good. The mailman never tapes anything to our door, nor do the neighbors. Only the property owner tapes paperwork to the door. This way, you can't say you didn't receive it. I hesitantly pull the envelope off the front door and walk back inside. I have a good idea of what's inside the envelope, and I'm scared to open it. I walk into the bathroom for privacy. I stand in front of the mirror and look at myself. Who have I become? I am a nervous wreck, with bad credit, no emergency fund, and no light in my face. The youthful spark in my eyes is gone. My face looks tired, worn down—without reason to smile. What have I done? How have I become this person?

After looking over my calculations of what we owe in back rent, I compare our total to that of the property owner and find that we owe more than what she has calculated. I respond with a letter to acknowledge our receipt of the Notice to Quit. I clarify the amount we owe and ask if we can pay down the balance by (maybe) having my husband make repairs on the building.

I finish writing the letter, pack the kids in the car, and drive fifteen minutes to the property owner's house. I surreptitiously park a few doors down from her house and quickly walk to her front porch. I quietly open the mailbox lid, drop the letter inside, and carefully close the lid, so she won't know I'm outside. A face-to-face conversation would be too uncomfortable and awkward. I can barely look myself in the eye. I hurry off the porch, get into the car, and return home. Throughout the evening, I anxiously go through our routine and wonder if she has checked her mailbox. Around 9:00 p.m., I get the kids into bed, wash the dinner dishes, and go into our bedroom to sit down to meditate.

As I sit in complete silence, my mind is unusually still. I affirm, "I happily pass this on. I am now free to be because I don't need to be in control of everything." I continue to sit in silence. I notice lightness moving around within me. I feel calm, with a sense of gratitude. I finally understand I need to give thanks in my darkest hour. I felt immense gratitude to know I do not need to bear this on my own; it is okay to release the burden of trying to figure out what to do. I don't need any more of my "plug the hole" tricks. In this moment, there is nothing else I alone can do. It is time to understand the difference between letting go and giving up.

In receiving the Notice to Quit, I will not try to "plug another hole". This is beyond my realm of tricks. I am tired, and weary, and have had enough of this mental fatigue. I am ready to let go.

For years, I've been trying to plug holes in a dam that would inevitably break. One "hole" represents the back-rent payments, another "hole" represents how to keep ourselves fed, and another is me trying to find a good work scenario. I am running around like a mouse in a maze, constantly asking myself, "What else should I do to change this? What more can be done?" I make desperate telephone calls to bill collectors and write letters to extend payment deadlines. I explain why I need help, and continue to ask in a state of anxiety. I recall that, one morning, I prayed to win the California Super Lotto. I thought "Maybe I haven't said 'please' enough times for my request to be granted." That morning, I sat on my bed for fifteen minutes and said, "Please, please, please, please, please, let me win the Super Lotto. Please, please…" Needless to say, I didn't win the lotto.

Now, of course, I'm not saying, when something of this nature occurs, that you should hide under the bed covers and release all personal responsibility. That's not what I did. I was unemployed and had been looking for work for an extensive period of time. For months, I would go to the local public library to use the computers to submit my resume online to open positions. To no avail, I applied to positions in which I was overqualified as well as those for which I was underqualified. I relentlessly applied to general administrative positions that were a match for my skills and qualifications. I even inquired about open positions for employment in person. However, I was routinely instructed to go online and submit the application. If you haven't had the experience of applying for work online, let me tell you, it seems hopeless. When you hit SEND or APPLY, it's like submitting your resume into a black hole where it is lost forever. More often than not, the only response I received was the following automated email response:

Dear BRIDGITTE,

Thank you very much for your recent submission of interest for the Administrative Assistant II opportunity. Your submission will be reviewed by our recruiting staff soon. Should we determine your qualifications are the best match for this position, we will contact you next. You can also check on the status of your submission by returning to our career site.

Thanks again for your interest and best of luck with your job search.

On some job boards, when you select a position to which you want to apply, you can see how many applicants have already applied for the same position. On one occasion, I looked at a particular administrative position with a well-known entertainment company. More than fifteen thousand applicants submitted for the position within the first week of the job posting! When I saw the number of applications already submitted, I couldn't believe that many people were looking for work in the same places I was. Several times, after having spent more than an hour going through an extensive application portal, I discovered that my application was around the two hundredth submission. Due to the influx of applications, several organizations began to state that applications would be accepted for a certain amount of time, and only on a specific date. For example, a secretary position within a local city government department posted the following notice on the Secretary job description page, "Applications will be accepted on November 10, 2011, beginning at 8:30 a.m. Applications will not be accepted after 10:00 a.m. on November 10, 2011, or once the first one hundred applications have been received." I had to schedule times on my calendar to remember to apply for positions. Looking for a job was a job within itself! And yes, I asked friends for referrals and whether they knew of companies that were hiring. On one occasion, my best friend referred me to a position at the company where she was a former full-time employee.

I email my resume for a Financial Compliance Administrative Assistant position to the Compliance Officer who will conduct the interview, and with whom I would work. After the initial telephone interview, we schedule an in-person interview for which I arrive on time and in my best professional attire. When I walk into the office, the Compliance Officer gives me a (very obvious) visual once-over and asks me to take a seat. She explains the details of the position, the inner workings of the company, her professional role, and the departmental structure. She goes into so much detail that the interview lasts for more than two hours! A few hours after the first in-person interview, I receive an email from the Compliance Officer. She enjoyed our interview. She asks me to write a letter to explain why I want to work with the company and what I will bring to the position. My cover letter already addressed this request, but I guess she wants to read it again. I write the letter and email it to her by 7:30 the next morning. Judging from her response two hours later, she loves it. One day later, I'm called for a second interview to meet my potential departmental coworkers. This interview lasts for three hours! Again, it goes well. However, as expected, the Compliance Officer is interviewing other candidates and needs a second opinion on prospective candidates. Two days after the second interview, I'm asked to come in for a *third* interview with the Vice President of the company. I can't believe how much I am being asked to do for an Administrative Assistant position that pays less than $30,000 a year. By now, four days have passed since my last interview. I have not heard anything from the Compliance Officer. My friend, who referred me to the company, has a conversation with the Compliance Officer to see how the hiring process for the position is coming along. The Compliance Officer casually tells my friend she is still conducting interviews, and she that got the impression I don't really want the job. What? After one telephone interview, three in-person interviews, a personal referral from my friend (her former colleague), a letter of interest, and five days of not hearing anything from the Compliance Officer, I rescind my application. Dealing with this song-and-dance over and over again is nothing less than discouraging, frustrating, and at times unfathomable. Somewhere along the way, while I was tending to children and under the impression I would easily find a job when ready, the hiring process changed. The job market is saturated with individuals who are just as qualified, hungry for work, and capable as I am. What is designed in the internet to make online applications accessible and convenient has become one of the biggest impediments. As a job seeker, I am in competition with candidates from all walks of life, and also dealing with hiring managers who act as if candidates need to be "rock stars." I have read many job descriptions that literally say, "We're looking for an administrative Rock Star..." Due to the lack of interview invitations, I also assume other candidates are better at getting their resumes past the software algorithms. Algorithms are designed to weed out candidates. Often, resumes are not viewed by a person. I'm not saying it is impossible to get a job. I'm saying the internet has completely changed the hiring landscape. Simply getting your resume in front of human eyes is a challenge. On top of this is the fact that you also have to deal with those who say, "...You don't really want a job because you don't have one. It just couldn't be that difficult. You could always work at McDonald's." There were times when I would give up for a while, and then start to look again.

Considering my husband works in the construction industry, which is still in the fallout of the economic downturn, it is extremely difficult to make the financial ends meet. He picks up jobs here and there, but work is inconsistent. He gets a job for a brief period of time and then goes for long stretches—weeks and sometimes months—without work. We remain in a perpetual state of trying to "catch up" on the bills and keep food on the table.

My main concern is, of course, our housing situation and the immediate crisis, but, beyond that, there is another layer underneath a continual situation of living in lack. Am I using this problem, or condition in my life, to reaffirm an addiction to fear or to being a victim? In addition to fully letting go, I also need to look at wounded parts of myself which have a more profound role in creating more financial dysfunction than I care to admit.

With the supportive pillow in place, I sit with my legs crossed, arms at ease on the top of my thighs, and palms up for receptivity. Once intuitively prompted, I begin with, "I call upon my Higher Self to join me in my meditation. During this meditation, I ask that you protect me from any and all vibrations, energies, frequencies, and communications in all directions of time, past, present, and future, that are not of love, light, and the highest good. Please let this communication be clear. Let the answers be communicated to me in a way that is easy for me to understand. Please let me feel your loving energy when you are ready to begin. I thank you in advance for your presence." Within a few moments, a slight surge of energy moves to the forefront of my awareness. A familiar lightness moves within me. It is time to begin.

This is the guidance that comes through:

Faith. *Let us begin by stating that the time of transition is upon you. You are being called to believe, with all that you are, in your path. Your path is laid before you and you have stepped onto it. You are being asked to take steps forward, without looking back. You are being asked to step forward, to let go and believe in something powerful that is unseen, but felt. You cannot, and you will not ever walk alone, but you must choose your direction…faith or fear. This is your time.*

Take a moment to feel your heart. What does it say? It says, "All is well," and that is your direction; the direction of love and wellness. Welcome it in.

Bless what you have experienced and all that you have learned. Know that you have learned the important and necessary parts of having faith, and dwelling in faith. Throughout all of these difficult times you are becoming whole and you are learning to love. No matter what is happening you are beginning to see that you are taken care of. With deep breaths, let the worry continue to flow out of your body. Worry flows out when you have had enough and are ready to trust in yourself.

No matter how difficult transitions may feel, they are vital in human and spiritual growth. You are stepping into growth, love, wisdom, and faith, all at once. We know what it is you want, what it is you seek in a life of financial ease. Let the blockages flow out of you that keep you stuck. Let them no longer hold space within your soul. Let your soul work how it was meant to work, in faith, love, service, and kindness. All lessons for the soul are difficult in the midst of resistance; and it is at the closing of the door of resistance that all becomes lighter. You are love, and loved, no matter what your earthly experiences are. Know that, as you are light shining through darkness, you are no longer the person you once were. You are love breaking through fear, and you are calm walking through the storm. So let it be. Times of uncertainty offer the greatest opportunity for growth and expansion. You are expanding. Open your heart, wide. Open your solar plexus and let the expansion in. It is happening. And do not worry about your children. They are loving souls. You are well and there is only love.

The deadline for the three-day Notice to Quit is tomorrow. I've been home all day with the kids, completing left-over homework, doing laundry, amidst a quiet acceptance of the situation. There will be no running around to see what I can sell, no frantic worrying, last-minute phone calls, or crying in the bathroom. Despite the fact that we are faced with having to move with no money, no credit, and no gas in the car, there is no anger and no sadness, only a slight discomfort. The discomfort is surrounded by a blanket of calm that reassures me that, no matter what happens, I will go on. We will go on. I will keep breathing and I will keep living, whether we are here or someplace else. I can no longer live with debilitating fear that something will happen that I cannot handle. Of course, a part of the concern is for our children. They are experiencing the results of our choices, beliefs, habits, and fears. I do not by any means want to uproot them without knowing where we will go, or how we will move forward. I do know that I can no longer let fear be the compass by which I decide what I will and can do. This must be what acceptance feels like.

Last week was a challenging week. It appeared as though my deepest fears were coming to pass. We had no money. It was difficult to feed ourselves and the kids as well as put gas in the cars. On two occasions, I drove around with the gas tank close to empty, praying, "Please let us arrive without running out of gas." In an effort to stretch what little gas remained in the tank, my driving was strategic to avoid any inclines or hills. So many times I wanted to ask for help, but I felt I shouldn't.

Toward the end of the week, on Sunday to be exact, I wake up with a strong feeling my mother is going to come over. Seeing that my cell phone has been disconnected, she can't call us. The feeling is so strong, I know she is thinking of us and we'll see her sometime today. Sure enough, around 3:00 p.m., not only does she ring the doorbell, but she comes bearing gifts! She brings bags of groceries and clothes for the kids. I am extremely grateful to see her walk in the door with love that encompasses her as a concerned grandmother, a caring mother, and gentle friend. At the same time, it is distressing that my life has come this.

Sunday is also the day our three-day Notice to Quit is due. We do not have the back rent payments, nor do we have money to move. I have not packed any of our belongings. After my Friday night meditation to move into acceptance of what is at hand, I have remained in a state of no resistance. As I move through the day, I continued to affirm my thoughts about what is going on. I affirm, "I know it is working out for my highest good and the highest good of all concerned. All is well. Believe and know it's already done." Feelings of acceptance and surrender now take up more space in my body than fear. It is hard, but I choose to trust the feelings of wellness. Periodically, doubt seeps in and I fear that I will have to find a homeless shelter for our family. In these moments of doubt, I direct my attention back to the feeling of wellness and surrender to a higher power. We are in a situation where we have no immediate solutions. However, although I cannot yet see it, I continue to believe something good is happening.

Late Sunday night, after my mother has left and the kids are asleep in bed, I sit down to check my email. There is an email from the property owner! In more fearful times, I would have left the unopened email in my inbox for hours while I worked up the nerve to open it and read it. Even after waiting, I would have closed one eye so I could peek at it one word at a time. This time is different. I immediately click to open the email. She agrees to consider letting Dennis do repairs around the building to work off the balance. We can stay. Thank you. Thank you. Thank you.

SUMMARY

What Is a Vision?

There is a difference between a vision and visualization. A visualization is when you mentally conceive and hold a known or familiar image in your mind. Whether we know it or not, we are continuously in a state of visualization, sometimes to our detriment. For example, although losing the house to foreclosure was not something I wanted to experience, for years I consistently held in my mind the idea of losing the house until it became a reality. The ongoing fearful emotional charge, coupled with holding the idea of losing the house, ultimately played a significant role in the outcome. I could visualize what losing the house would look like because I could mentally conceive foreclosure.

A vision, on the other hand, is an idea, inspiration, goal, or dream that seeks to manifest into reality through you. A vision is something you allow, something that calls to you specifically because you are the conduit for the expression. A vision is not necessarily something you will have an immediate image to represent in your mind. It can be a feeling that continues to prompt and urge you. For example, throughout the financial turmoil, I often felt prompted to write. For many reasons, and for some time, I ignored the internal prompts. However, the idea of writing simply would not go away. In the beginning, I didn't have any idea of what I should write, to whom I should write, on which online platform, or if I could write anything someone would read. All I know is that the urge was there. The urge, or prompting, serves to validate that the fundamental roots of the vision are already in place within you. It is through by following through on the inspired action you are prompted to take that you begin to align your life with the vision. For example, let's say the vision that wants to emerge through you is for you to start a charity organization of some kind, but you don't have the money. The vision may then prompt you to begin by aligning yourself with a mentality of abundance. You may be urged to get the money you do have available in order. You may be prompted to thoroughly examine the following: your spending habits, the expectation of not having enough money, or the feeling of panic you get with unexpected expenses. Initially, it may not seem as though the promptings are related to the vision, but remember, the vision builds upon itself one piece, one step, and one intention at a time. This building, if you will, of the vision will call for a sacred type of discipline and patience that can alter your way of being, and help you pull away from the mental constraints of limitation.

A vision can expand your awareness and ultimately have an effect on your actions. As you become more adept at identifying the highest course of action from a perspective of clarity and inspiration, the vision can help you to begin to create from a place independent of fear. Clarity around the vision can help you determine which actions to follow. As you continue to actualize inspiration through inspired action, the vision will continue to build upon itself. This is why you don't need to have everything figured out to start taking action towards the vision. You have to trust that you are being led onto your highest path through the following:

1. Let the Vision Reveal Itself

To have new experiences in your life, you have to be willing to have new ideas in your conscious awareness. If you're not sure where to begin, you can begin by asking contemplative questions to identify what is trying to get your attention and connect with you. The contemplative questions can help to hone in on the vision. In the bigger picture, not only can the vision help you clarify who you want to become, and who you are meant to become, but also what wants to be experienced, created, and contributed through you.

Once seated in a quiet place where you are comfortable and relaxed, and can remain undisturbed, write down the first question and let the answer reveal itself to you. Pay attention to the first thing that comes into your awareness. If there is no immediate answer for a question, you can try again at another time, meditate on the question, and then move on to the next one. Remember, there is no right or wrong answer, only clarity.

Contemplative Questions:

1. What vision do I have that, no matter how long I ignore it, won't go away?

2. Does the vision originate in my heart or in my head?

3. Am I curious about the vision? Do I want to find out or know more?

4. Does the vision feel purposeful?

5. Does the vision require me to compromise my personal integrity or authenticity?

6. What do I want to contribute to my family, my community, and the world that would make me feel proud, honorable, and content?

7. Am I letting the vision come from within, or am I trying to create it in my mind?

8. Is any part of the vision based on an underlying secret desire for approval?

From the written answers to the contemplative questions, form a paragraph to see what has been revealed to you. This does not have to be done in one sitting. It may take several sessions of listening and contemplation to gain clarity around the vision. Some aspects will be clear, while other aspects may take more time. You will need to use your own discernment to determine whether you have honed in on the vision. When you feel you are clear, the next question is: How do you hold the vision?

2. Hold the Vision

What does it mean to hold the vision? It means you continually hold the idea, aspiration, goal, or dream in your mind. You hold the vision in your mind so that the awareness of the vision allows you to recognize signs, directional confirmation, encouragement, and guidance that indicate you and your actions are in alignment to manifest the vision—signs that you're moving in the right direction. You will intuitively recognize information (guidance) that is meant for you. You will start to realize things without trying and suddenly have insights that seem to come out of nowhere. I once spoke with Leah Pearlman (Dharma Comics) about where her creative ideas come from. She said, "It's almost like the idea was in the street and I just walked into it." The information (guidance) can come to you in many ways, such as through thoughts, dreams, ideas, feelings, people, signposts, songs, etc., and it will touch you and stay with you for some time. It will touch you because it is resonating with you. The resonance indicates the information "speaks" to you in a way that is meaningful. You will know it was meant for you. When you hold the vision, you are focusing your awareness on purpose. Within this focus, you can become clear on the intentional role you have in co-creating what you want to create, and what wants to be created through you.

How to hold the vision:

○ Continually hold the vision (idea, aspiration, goal, or dream) to remain in affirmation that you are aware of the vision.

○ The awareness of the vision will inspire you to recognize pertinent messages to take personal action.

○ Engaging in inspired action creates momentum in the belief that the vision is possible.

○ The vision ultimately emerges in your life, or as your life.

How to nurture the vision:

○ Trust the vision.

○ Believe in the vision.

○ Create a feeling of belief in your body to allow space for the vision to grow.

○ Ask your internal Higher Intelligence to move you in the right direction, to connect with the right people and situations.

○ Act upon inspirational thoughts, feelings, and ideas related to the vision.

○ Know that inspired action is trying to move you in the direction of the vision.

○ Know the vision is an expression of love.

What sabotages the vision?

○ When doubt is stronger than belief.

○ Complaining. This holds your attention on what you say you don't want.

○ Rumination over fearful thoughts. This chips away at the foundation of the belief.

○ Rumination over doubtful thoughts. This chips away at the possibility of the life and vision becoming a reality.

3. Trust the Vision

To have trust in the vision will call for a shift in your thinking and beliefs. It will require that you enlarge your perspective about your life and what you believe is possible. You will have to abandon attachment to the small perception of your life and move to embrace the idea of vast possibilities. It will require a deep examination of your accumulated beliefs to determine which beliefs are self-sabotaging and which are life-enhancing. From where you stand, you cannot know all the possibilities available to you. It's like an ant trying to have perspective on the world; you can only see what you can see from where you are, according to what you know. However, you *can* have trust in the vision that, as you are willing to hold a larger perspective, helpful people and unforeseen opportunities will find you. The shift in thinking will call for you to know that you are a part of a Higher Intelligence, and that this intelligence is within you and speaks to you. It is up to you to decide if you will strengthen your ability to hear and listen, and then decide what you will do with the guidance you have been given.

Holding trust in the vision will also require you to use discernment regarding information that comes into your awareness. Remember, "Believe what your body tells you is true." How does your body speak to you? Through the soul center.

As you develop discernment, you will be able to better identify how truthful information feels within your body.

Here are suggestions to identify how truthful information feels within your body:

○   Bring your attention to the place within your body where intuition is felt the most strongly.

○   Ask the following questions:

1. Does this feel true for me?

2. Does my body recognize truth in this information?

As you ask your question, pay attention to your body and feel the answer come into your awareness. This will help you to identify what it feels like when information comes into your soul center, or mind, and the difference in the feeling between the two. Ultimately, you will use your mind, your soul center, and your heart to work together in a complementary and unified way.

4. Surrender

Surrender can be perceived as one of the most difficult parts of growth. It can easily be confused with a feeling of powerlessness. The idea of not doing something, anything, to address a problem seems to go against your very nature. However, surrender does not mean that you give up, stop trying, or relinquish your sense of power. It is precisely the opposite. Surrender means you relax into acceptance of where you are and what is happening. You allow yourself to *experience* the feeling of powerlessness you associate with surrender and accumulated defeats. You don't have to like what is happening, but it is within surrender that you choose to release your "death grip" attachment to what you want, think, or believe should happen. When you've exhausted all mental, emotional, and physical resources and attempts at situational manipulation to no avail, you've come to the end of resistance. When you stop resisting, the tension and angst within your body and around the situation subsides. All is quieted, and the solution-oriented energy can move. The energy can begin to shift on your behalf because now you are receptive. It is within surrender that you realize you can let go; that there is power is letting go. You don't have to figure it all out. You can be willing to acknowledge that just because you can't see an outcome, that does not mean nothing is happening.

Here are suggestions to encourage surrender:

○ Know that you don't have to agree with or like what is happening, but you can change your response.

○ Relax into acceptance of where you are and what is happening.

○ Breathe and meditate to help your body release the tension and emotional charge around the concern.

○ If you are unsure of what to do next, be still.

○ Be still and know that life is not against you, it is for you.

5. Faith

Faith is to believe in something felt, but unseen. You can have situational faith, or you can dwell in faith. Often, we speak of having faith when something difficult, uncertain, or frightening comes about. During such times, we say, "Just have faith." And that's okay, but faith is not only to be experienced momentarily, when we are most in need of faith. You can choose to dwell in faith. You can employ sacred discipline to stand in faith even when all is well, or when

something is moderately concerning, as well as during the darkest of times.
When you let faith hold you, you walk in courage with an advocate of wellness.

Here are suggestions to dwell in faith:

○   With deep breaths, inhale the feelings of love and wellness.

○   On the exhale, breathe out whatever is worrisome at that moment.

○   Let the worry continue to flow out of your body.

○   Continue to do this until you feel more at ease.

○   Think of a prayer that speaks directly to your heart. Say this prayer as much as you need to throughout the day to anchor the energy of the Higher Presence and love.

Breath and prayer does sound very simple, maybe too simple (you might think) for large scale problem(s). However, breathing and prayer have a calming, loving, and anchoring effect that can help when you are in need.

THE GIFT OF CRISIS

CHAPTER THREE

CHANGE IS SIMPLY CHANGE

I wake up this morning at 5:43 a.m. As my eyes open, I begin a prayer to give thanks for the seen and unseen support and blessings in my life. After prayer, I don't get out of bed. I don't want to let my feet hit the floor just yet. By staying in the quietude of silence for as long as I can, I'll delay the rush of reality setting in. The kids are still asleep, and I won't wake them for another thirty minutes. This undisturbed time, along with the stillness of late-night hours, has become a relished part of my day. During this time, no bill collectors contact me for payment. There are no FedEx deliveries of judgments, envelopes from credit collectors, or unexpected knocks on the front door from gas company employees. For as long as I remain underneath the covers, I am alone with intact hope. Maybe today I will receive an email requesting that I come in for the job interview. Maybe today Dennis will start work on a room addition. Maybe. Or maybe today will be the day I finally decide to give up, stay here beneath the comfort of the covers, and hide behind drawn shades from the dilemmas for which I have no immediate solutions. One week has passed since the scare over our housing situation. Although that situation is temporarily addressed, there remains the reality of how to deal with day-to-day expenses that arise.

It is now close to 6:15 a.m. The roar of buses passing outside on the street and cars rushing by interrupt the silence. It is time to face reality. I sit on the edge of the bed and reluctantly look at the floor. Before my feet land on the carpet, I remember there is very little gas in the car. Here we go again.

My husband is gone. He left early to cover a friend's newspaper delivery route. Dennis and I barely talk beyond what is necessary. It is all we can do to avoid yelling and screaming at each in front of the kids. With extreme financial uncertainty now an invasive third wheel in our marriage, blame and resentment taints most, if not all, of our interactions and conversations. Instead of Dennis and me demonstrating emotional maturity and trying to find a way to uphold each other, we withdraw into individual protective cocoons as if to say "every man for himself." With financial threat constantly looming, we are both afraid. Also stimulating fear is the fact that Dennis is angry with me. He is angry that he carries the pressures of the financial burden. He is angry about facing the possibility that he may not rise to the occasion of taking care of the family. On a deeper level, I think he is also angry that I have not become the person he thought I would. I have a college degree; therefore, it is expected that I will be in the professional lead. He is angry that instead of me taking *any* job I can find, I talk about needing to find a job that will not only allow me to contribute financially but also pay for after-school care for the kids. Gavin is four years-old and attends preschool three days a week. It is during Gavin's time at preschool that I schedule interviews, complete online applications at the library, and write articles for Examiner. To take a full-time position, which I want, means we will have to increase his enrollment to five days a week and pay for after-school classes for Greyson and Mckenna. If I don't find a job that pays more than these extra costs, my entire paycheck will again be absorbed by childcare fees. We've already been down this road when I worked at USC while Mckenna was in preschool. But that argument doesn't resonate with him as anything other than an excuse. This is a profound difference in the way he and I view this scenario. He doesn't care where I work, or what I need to do, as long as I hold up my end of paying half of the bills. My contemptuous response is, "Funny how the bills need to be equally divided, but not the housework, doctor visits, dental exams, and all those other 'unimportant, paperwork-type things.'" My main concern is not to buy a new car every five years, but that our children are well cared for by trusted adults. I'm not saying I don't want the benefits that come with a high and steady income. Who doesn't want that? However, I am concerned about our children being in a safe and trusted environment. Why am I the one who has to choose between work and children? Why am I the one trying to figure out what will happen to the kids while I work? On some days, however, I do have second thoughts. Maybe childcare isn't as important as I make it out to be. But then I talk with my mommy friends, one who told me about her toddler being given Benadryl to make him go to sleep while at day care, or another who arrived at the childcare center only to find the diaper was so drenched the toddler's bottom had begun to chafe. Maybe my concern is influenced by the fact that I went to pick up my son, from a sister-in-law's house, to find him with a busted lip. My goal is to find work that allows me to pay for a quality after-school environment, in addition to our living expenses, and, if I'm really lucky, is also meaningful and conducive to family. Both of our concerns are equally important, and it doesn't serve anyone's highest interest for Dennis and me to lean in opposite directions. I know that I will have a hard time concentrating on any job if I am not secure with childcare. On the other hand, I also know it is difficult for Dennis to concentrate on finding work, and doing a good job at the work site, if he worries we will never dig ourselves out of this financial hole. Without good jobs held by both of us, this is an impossible situation.

On many occasions, I have thought that perhaps I did make the wrong decision to stay home with Mckenna. Maybe I was irresponsible for having a third child in the midst of this crisis. In hindsight, it was my lack of planning and foresight that led to this inevitability. In staying home with Mckenna, I made the decision to put the children before my financial responsibilities and before my marriage. I made the decision to opt out of the workforce after being laid off from teaching, thus severely damaging my earning potential and employability. Yes, it was financially irresponsible to prolong being at home with Mckenna for so long that it became difficult to get a job. As selfish as it may have been, I wanted to do it. I wanted to be with her and care for her. I wanted to be with them. I believed that, because we were young, we had plenty of time to earn and save money, to buy a house and do all the things that having great incomes would afford. What we would not have is a second opportunity to raise our children. The early developmental years pass quickly, and that was the time for me, for us, to instill and impress upon them qualities and experiences of unconditional love. Despite the enormity of problems intertwined within this decision, and the complexity of emotional wounds it brought to the surface, the small piece of comfort I now garner is that our children appear to be well-adjusted. Although they're still being raised, I can already see that they are each kind, respectful, fun, and sweet and still move within the joy of unhindered possibility.

I make it to both the elementary school and middle school and back home without running out of gas. I unlock the front door, walk inside and sit in the middle of the sofa in what has become my "poor me" spot. I look around the living room as warm sunlight filters in through the blinds and spreads rays of light across the carpet. I hear birds chirping outside and decide this is as good a spot as any to begin meditation.

I scoot all the way back on the sofa and place a pillow behind my back. I cross my legs, let my arms relax with my palms facing up, and close my eyes.

I yearn for silence beyond what I had this morning, during the quiet hours. I am developing a much-needed and wanted relationship with silence. The silence drowns out the mental and emotional noise. It encourages me to slow down and gather myself. Meditation is quickly becoming something I have to have.

I take a long breath in through my nose and with my mouth slightly agape, slowly let it out. I feel my body relax. In through the nose, out through the mouth, and I relax even more. I take in another breath and amplify space around me. I stay with my breath and heartbeat and sink deeper into myself. The feeling of my arms, legs, and chest fade into the background of my awareness, and I continue to move inward. For this moment, everything outside of me becomes superfluous. No words drift by, and no thoughts push through. I rest in this space of timelessness. I hold onto silence, and time slips away with each breath. After what I imagine are several minutes, a feeling of "wanting to know" wells inside of me. I take another long breath and, like clouds drifting across an afternoon sky, my words to call in guidance drift into my awareness:

"I call upon my Higher Self to join me in my meditation. During this meditation, I ask that you protect me from any and all vibrations, energies, frequencies, and communications in all directions of time, past, present, and future, that are not of love, light, and the highest good. Please let this communication be clear. Let the answers be communicated to me in a way that is easy for me to understand. Please let me feel your loving energy when you are ready to begin. I thank you in advance for your presence."

I'm familiar with all the sensations I normally associate with my physical body during a meditative state. As I wait for guidance, there is a consistency to the subtle flow of energy moving within me. The energy is smooth, steady, light, and uninterrupted, like a gentle spring breeze. Words began to softly arise into my awareness.

This is the guidance that comes through:

Change. *You are now in clear understanding that change is simply change. It is not to be viewed as negative or positive. It is simply change. There is no disappointment, no reward for good behavior, no end result of "you've finally won." There is only change. It is not necessary to view it from a perspective of goodwill bestowed upon you because of worthiness. It is change, and change is always meant to equal and cause growth. Know that growth and development are central to spiritual and energetic completions. You are not meant to stagnate. You are meant to have experiences that initiate and call for growth. After growth comes service, because you are called to share what you have learned along the way. You are called to give what you have learned to others in any manner that is aligned with goodness. You are upon change and change is upon you. Know that you are loved and we are with you always.*

Let fearful beliefs disintegrate. *We are here. As we have previously spoken about this moment in your life, when meeting the basic needs of your family is difficult, it is serving to strip away your insecurities, doubts, and fearful beliefs that your basic needs are not met, were not met. This experience is disintegrating that belief within you. For so long, this belief of not having enough has held space within your body and your energy field. It has brought the most primal need to the surface for healing. The doubts and misperceptions are fading away, like sand when you stand up at the beach. The sand sticks to you for as long as it is able. When it can no longer stick, it falls away. It is the same with sabotaging beliefs about yourself and your world. You can also think of it as glue being pulled off your skin (like you used to do as a child); you let it dry, then you peeled it off slowly so the entire piece would remain intact. It is the same now with the old, destructively fearful energies. They are slowly peeling away. As there is less attached to you that holds you in fear, you feel lighter and "feel" your way, through your body, into the new. You are being called to live authentically in touch with who you really are.*

Let the universe support you. *Look for support. Declare examples of support and remain in gratitude. Remain. You are loved and your life is moving and shifting to reflect this for you. You are moving towards being able to see that you are worthy, your needs are met, you were not abandoned, and you are a reflection of the love that surrounds you. You are finding that you are taken care of and you are supported. Support may not come in the way that you or society indicates is okay, but you are supported. Look around you.*

Let the experience flow. *Continue to move through with no resistance. Let it move beyond you. Keep your body as unrestrictive as you can. When your body is clenched and tight, you keep the experience you do not want close to you; you create more of it. Release it by letting your body remain open and relaxed. Know that you are blessed, even though it may not feel so …you are blessed. Remain delighted to know that as a caterpillar emerges into a beautifully unmatched butterfly, so are you undergoing transformation to emerge as a beautiful being. Know this to be true. Remain in awareness that the experience of life, abundance, brilliance, curiosity, hope, and faith can only flow through you if you remain unclenched.*

Feel your intuition move you along your life path. Use your mind to complement what is true for you.

Tonight, I attended a free prayer workshop at the spiritual center and learned a different approach to prayer. According to the workshop facilitator, prayer is not solely to be used for the purpose of asking for something, but also to affirm that whatever it is you seek is already available to you. Prayer is the means through which the energy around an event, or circumstance, can shift as you affirm and declare that there is a Higher Intelligence available for us to connect with as we turn within. Deeply sincere and heartfelt prayer is a soft, intimate, and endearing language of the soul that serves as an invocation for blessing, healing, guidance, help, and protection. When you speak in a manner of sincere reverential prayer, you engage acceptance and surrender. Within acceptance and surrender, you deepen your relationship to love, faith, humility, gratitude, and compassion, all of which are qualities that direct us toward the Higher Presence that permeates all.

For the majority of my life, I believed a majestic power outside of myself could intervene, remedy the problem or situation, or just make everything alright, if I asked and begged with enough fervor. I'm now in a different place. With continued spiritual reading and meditation, I now believe in an all-encompassing Higher Intelligence that I have access to from within. When I pray, I reach within, and my Higher Self connects to this all-encompassing Intelligence. Prayer and meditation are practices I use to create an internal environment within me, which expands the reach of my consciousness to connect with this Higher Intelligence.

When I got into bed later that night and positioned myself for meditation, again I held the intention for more clarity.

This is the guidance that came through:

Be open to life. *You are opening up to life. You are opening up to patience, divine timing, and flow. You are taking right actions by believing in what you seek. You believe in your visualizations and act from this place of knowingness. This is what you can and should do. Stones you cast months ago, through efforts for meaningful work, are ready to be met. Your job is to let it be, to let it come to your surface eyes. You have felt that things need to move faster, but also you understand that change may not be the end of all things as a result of your desires not manifesting "quickly" enough. Your needs continue to be met. You are in the "unknown" yet known spot of life. It is possible to be open to life, all the while knowing that what you expect (meaningful work) has come to you. The gift of being open to life is that you are certain of what you would like to come, but it will come in a manner that you could have never anticipated. Beautiful, is it not? Simply beautifully orchestrated because it all is for your highest good.*

<u>You once felt awkward about showing love, and wondered why someone would love you so much.</u> *Many see what you cannot. Many can feel love within you making its way to the surface. You now see and feel that there is no vulnerability. There is no vulnerability in letting people love you and showing them how much you love them. There is love. You are love and it must be given and received. Let it flow. Smile, laugh, and express joy, because your life is blossoming into fullness as you blossom into love. This is a momentous time. You are here to show the expansion and to experience the expansion. Your grass is becoming green. You do not need to look across the street, or anywhere else. Yours is in the "green." Love. There is only love for you.*

For months, I attended free talks, seminars, workshops, and presentations geared toward spirituality. I wanted to learn as much as I could about how to practically apply spiritual practice in my life and encourage personal growth. It was through attendance at a particular workshop that I became aware of Dr. Sue Morter and heard her speak for the first time.

Dr. Morter specializes in integrative work around energy fields and energy centers in the body. She teaches how deep breathing can be used to work with energy and initiate healing to allow access to higher frequencies and potentials. Through the workshop, I began learning how to move energy. During the presentation, Dr. Morter explained, "Breathing helps to transmute energy to work for you, rather than against you. Wanting to 'get rid' of something comes from 'living in your head,' and nothing can be transformed there. Breathing helps to move your consciousness deeper inside your body and out of your head, where worry takes place. You have to use the other aspects of your whole being, such as your body, to ground and transform anything. When you breathe deep from within the belly, instead of the chest, the nervous system goes into healing mode. Sustainable change happens in the body." Dr. Morter teaches that one has to "work with the energy, not the "story," by "moving the energy of your life with your breath." What? "Change happens in the body?" I had never heard this before, but, as I have come to recognize, the body knows truth, as the words resonated with my soul center. Your body intuitively recognizes words, actions, sentiments, and deeds of truth. If you are in tune with your soul center and validate it as being intuitively intelligent, you begin to tune into your body to determine whether outside information resonates with truth. When I hear, see, or feel outside information, I immediately pay attention to how it moves through my body. I have found that information will initiate an energetic sensation of either a strong "yes" or a resounding "no." What is important is to be clear if I'm tuned into my intuitive soul center, or if I'm tuned into fear-based emotions. You have to be clear on how to delineate between the two. When I heard the words, "change happens in the body," I knew she spoke truth.

Given that all I think of is our dire financial situation and how unbelievably unsuccessful my job search is, it is clear I am absolutely identified with my story. The meditation sessions, books, talks centered on spiritual and personal growth and finding communal support all help along the way. Every time I hear someone speak at a seminar, I write down what resonates within me as truth and make a sincere and concerted effort to integrate the advice or practice into my life. It isn't easy, and I'm not always successful, but all of it helps.

What stuck with me from Dr. Morter's talk is what I most need to hear, "You can stand in love, while having a 'bad' experience. You don't need to love the situation, but BE in love where you are." It took years for me to fully comprehend the gravity of this statement. We don't have to like where we are in life, the conditions of our present circumstance, or situations in which we find ourselves surrounded. But we can still harbor a Higher Presence of love. We can choose to allow ourselves to rest in love instead of anger and resentment.

In the days that followed Dr. Morter's talk, before going into silence during meditation, I began with this prayer. This is a personalized template for affirmative prayer that I wrote during the prayer workshop so I could refer to it often:

MY PRAYER OF GRATITUDE

I am grateful for life, and my life.

I am grateful for all the experiences and circumstances that have brought me to where I am today,

because in this space, I am more awake than I was yesterday.

I am grateful for my husband who (in his own way) pushes me to choose faith over fear.

I am grateful for my eldest son who reminds me to give love and find comfort in receiving love.

I am grateful for my daughter who helps me to remember creativity, self-expression, and the inner

knowingness that comes with being firmly planted within truth.

I am grateful for my youngest son who shows me what joy looks like when it is a way of being.

I recognize that I could not have arrived at this place of compassion, non-judgment and presence had I not forgotten so much during my life.

As life unfolds in love, I unfold in love.

I am thankful now that I am willing to begin again.

I continue to let it be.

And so it is.

Following prayer, I begin meditation. This time it is easy to slip into stillness. Little by little, it's getting easier. There are still times when I struggle to maintain the silence, but the thoughts are becoming less intrusive and less forceful. They are still there, trying to make themselves heard, but it is getting easier for me to let them float into the background without trying hard to do so.

The kids are asleep in bed, and Dennis is asleep on the sofa with the television watching him. In order to have quiet, I have to get up, once again, and walk into the living room to turn down the volume. It never ceases to amaze me how loud the volume is when he watches television. I repeatedly (and strongly) suggest that he turn on the damn subtitles and turn down the volume. He says, "The subtitles require too much work. I don't want to "work" when I'm watching TV." I have resorted to frequently walking into the living room, grabbing the remote and turning down the television in the middle of one of his National Geographic Wild animal shows without saying one word to him. Now, when he hears me coming into the living room, he quickly grabs the remote, and sits on top of it to keep me from grabbing it. He continues to watch the TV without looking at me, as if I'm not standing there staring at him. It's ridiculous. Tonight, I leave the television on with the volume at a whisper, place a blanket over him, and return to my meditative position on the bed. Nighttime and early morning are wonderful times for meditation because it's so quiet. No traffic noise from the street, no blaring emergency sirens, and no neighbors blasting their music or Dennis blasting the television. There is only silence and me. I get comfortable in my seated position with my pillow, prayer of gratitude, pen, and notepad in hand. My legs, arms, back, and entire body are becoming more and more familiar with this posture and what is to come. I read my prayer of gratitude out loud to move deeper into gratitude. After the prayer, I close my eyes and continue to feel the presence of gratitude. I wonder what information will arise as a result of this gratitude. I already have a question in mind, so I move straight to meditative guidance.

"I call upon my Higher Self to join me in my meditation. During this meditation, I ask that you protect me from any and all vibrations, energies, frequencies, and communications in all directions of time, past, present, and future, that are not of love, light, and the highest good. I ask that you look deeply into my heart to know my aspirations for my family and my life, so I may receive guidance to bring these visions into my reality. Please let this communication be clear. Let the answers be communicated to me in a way that is easy for me to understand. Please let me feel your loving energy when you are ready to begin. I thank you in advance for your presence."

Within silence, I hold the intention to know, "What is needed of me to begin to manifest the job that is aligned with my soul's purpose?"

This is the guidance that came through:

Create the pathway for expansion. *Whether it is a change you had hoped for or a change you did not expect, the time has come, and change comes to everyone when they are truly ready. Keep stepping toward growth, keep writing, keep expecting, and keep affirming you have learned the vital aspects of prayer. Let your eyes see this, let your body feel this, and your mind will find a way to bring the visualization to the forefront. It is only you. You will bring this forth. Believe it first, and then see it. It is you, so let it be. The stripping away of all you held onto, to identify with, has begun the cleansing.*

There can be no more distractions. You are here at the precipice of stepping through another doorway to yourself and your being. You but need to walk through and close the door behind you. Seek because what you seek is moving you into being, growth, and love. You are here for this. Be light, be strength, be love, and know that you are learning to love yourself. You are remembering that all beings of sacredness are to be honored. You are in this world because you knew you would remember. You knew the purpose would be fulfilled. Be it. Be what you are and trust. Trust your body. All parts of yourself dwell in your body. Let the parts integrate. Let them love you. Do not be discouraged, or "deflated" (as you say). It is at the point of release that you let go and allow a higher source to intervene. Let go. Let us help you help yourself. You are desperately wanting movement, change, a new stage of life. We feel this. You have undergone a tremendous amount of spiritual growth that will not allow you to fall backwards. **Maintain a state of calm.**

From where you are now, there is only realization and
understanding that you must uphold certain elements in your life:
faith, compassion for yourself and others, belief, love for all that
is, and maintaining a state of being calm. The discomfort will not
vanish, but you will begin to see uncomfortable circumstances with
fresh eyes. It's all for growth. It's all for spiritual advancement to
your purpose. It's all to help you remember your reach, your power,
your loving state, and your abilities. Nothing has been taken away
from you, not even during your darkest hour; all has been given to
you. You have but to see. **Believe it, then see it.** See the life you
seek to create. See the marriage you seek to experience. SEE the
existence you seek when not only you, but all, exist in cooperation,
harmony, care, and love for one another. It is possible, all of this
is possible, and it is beginning. Remember, change is change. It
begins with one step creating the way for others to join in. So join
your life. Join the growth. Join the transcendence of all that is
dismantling within your body and within your world. Great change
is upon you all. You must know and accept that you are here to
be a part of this change. All along there have been small, but
consistent, changes within all of you that are now initiating and
contributing to global change. There is only love.

SUMMARY

Change

Change is often viewed as something unwanted, uncertain, and uncontrollable. In fact, for some, merely hearing the word "change" causes some level of distress. When change is one that is pre-determined as being a "wanted change," like winning the Super Lotto, buying your dream house, or securing a highly coveted professional contract, change does not feel threatening. With "wanted change", these are circumstances we consider familiar, routine, acceptable, and controllable. We think we know what life will entail because we assume we know what life will look like within this type of change. However, change is not always comfortable, but it is necessary, because the only constant is change. Life is energy, and energy is always changing. We resist change because the fear *is* resistance. Our mind is always looking for patterns and boxes to keep us safe. Although you may feel that you come out of safety when you allow change to take place, your safety is more attached to your ability to allow change and to adapt. When you acknowledge how you have coped with change thus far, the fact that you are reading this book means you are being called to something else…to change.

Change is fundamental to growth, and there will and should always be change. That means you let the fearful thoughts disintegrate and keep "putting one foot in front of the other" even when you're terrified, and even when you don't know what will happen. You can let the universe support you by bringing a new experience into your life. When change is moving you in the direction of your highest good, you will know, and in this knowing you may still feel a bit unsettled. However, coupled with a sincere desire for something better in your life, change can lead you exactly where you are most needed and exactly where you need to go.

Key points to remember regarding change:

○ Life, in and of itself, is change.

○ Change is not to be viewed as negative or positive, but instead as simply change.

○ Change is always meant to equal and cause growth.

○ Change helps you move out stagnation.

○ You are meant to have experiences that initiate and call for growth.

○ During moments of resistance, there will always be an "exit" to encourage the stagnant energy to break up.

○ Change is not separate from support. The solution and the answer are always in the same place.

○ After growth comes service. Share what you have learned in any manner aligned with goodness to benefit others.

Contemplative Questions:

1. What is it about change that frightens me?

2. What is it about change that makes me feel uncomfortable or unsafe?

3. Do I have to know what comes next?

4. Do I believe the universe is for or against me?

5. If I'm not satisfied with the way things are in my life, where does my resistance to change come from?

6. Am I willing to be open to new experiences, people, and ways of being?

7. Have I ever gone through a difficult change and come out stronger?

8. Where in my life do I stop change from happening?

9. How can I create forward movement in a situation that has the appearance of stagnation or blockage?

10. At the moment of great change, what is the thing that (consistently) happens to keep me stuck where I am?

11. What is it within me that will allow me to take the next step when I feel afraid?

12. During a current moment of change, am I able to recognize the presence of grace?

1. Let Fearful Beliefs Disintegrate

Fearful and self-sabotaging beliefs cannot be addressed until you recognize they are having substantial effects on your life. It took years of experiencing a situation of financial lack for me to finally recognize I harbored the unconsciousness beliefs that my needs are not met, that there is not enough to go around, and that I cannot give anything to anyone because I will not have enough. This entire line of thinking stemmed from a mentality of lack, i.e., "I do not have what I need, I will not get what I really want, and I am not taken care of." This is a powerful and extremely self-negating vibration to continually send out into the world. Through reading, I have come to understand the universe meets us where we are. Like attracts like due to energetic vibration; therefore, if I whole-heartedly believe that I do not have enough and will not get what I truly want or need, my outer experience will reflect my internal beliefs. I unconsciously look for validation of these beliefs. In this manner of thinking, I was heavily identified with, and attached to, the smallest and most frightened parts of myself.

When you understand thoughts are simply thoughts, you also understand you do not have to believe everything you think about yourself. What you believe is only as true as you believe it to be, regardless of whether it is encouraging or discouraging.

There is no need for self-imposed suffering due to a limited perception of ourselves. We are so much more than fear and doubt, so much more than the limited perceptions we harbor of ourselves. We are, in fact, deeply complex beings who are tethered to love, light, and wholeness. As you begin to know that you do not have to live a life dictated by fearful perceptions, fear will take up less space in your life. It will not completely go away, as it can be useful, but it will take up less space. It will play a less prominent role in how you respond, what you think, what you believe, and the actions you take.

Contemplative Questions:

1. Ask yourself, "What is the underlying cause of this fear?" When you respond, ask yourself again what the underlying cause of this fear is. Continue to drill down until you get to the core of the fear. This may require that you ask the above question several times. You will know when you have uncovered the core fear. (*Ex. I don't have enough. I am not safe. I am not secure.*)

2. Ask yourself, "What is the fundamental message within this fear?" What is the fear trying to tell you? (*Ex. I can choose to believe that I have enough, that I am safe and secure. I can look for external validation to affirm this belief. I can act in ways that demonstrate belief in my personal wellness. I can choose to relax and soften the energy around this fear.*)

How to let fearful thoughts disintegrate:

○ When fear arises, acknowledge the fearful energy in your body and take note of where fear resides in your body. (*Note: Feel the discomfort of fear in your body without dwelling on it. You are simply acknowledging its existence.*)

○ Take slow and deep breaths to calm yourself. (*Note: Do not underestimate the power of intentional breathing. "Breathing helps to move your consciousness down inside your body, and out of your head where worry takes place."*)

○ Mentally examine the cause that triggers the fear by asking the two contemplative questions. (*Note: With practice, you will become adept at quickly identifying emotional triggers.*)

○ Peel back the topical "layers" of what you *tell* yourself the fear is about, and do the "heavy lifting" of really looking at what lies beneath the fear.

- Be honest with yourself on what the fear is *really* about.

- Take personal responsibility for knowing you have a choice about how you choose to respond.

- Know there is power within you to respond from a place of courage, self-empowerment, and faith.

- Choose to recognize and acknowledge all forms of abundance around you.

- Know that, as you release fear, you realign with truth.

- Express gratitude for clarity.

2. Let the Universe Support You

The universe is always trying to communicate with you, always seeking to support you. Your task is to pay attention, to recognize the language in which the universe speaks to you, and extract the personal message of what is relayed to you within the "good" or "bad" experience. Messages are communicated to you repeatedly until you recognize and understand them. Remember, because you are one with the universe and are tethered to a Higher Intelligence, messages on your behalf will resonate with you. The possibilities for ways the universe supports you are boundless. Synchronicities, helpful people, problems which lead to blessings in disguise, a phone call from just the right person, surprisingly wonderful outcomes, support groups, a stranger who delivers a profound message to you, entertainment, challenges, and grace are but a few examples of how the universe communicates support for you. Support may not come in the manner you expect, or prefer, but nevertheless, support is there. You constantly receive cues from words and images that you can use to help you cross an invisible (mental) bridge during a moment of change. For me, change does not always feel like a blissful ride down a sunlit canal. Sometimes I need additional help. In addition to meditation and prayer, I also like to utilize movie scenes. For example, a visual image that greatly assists me to navigate fearful moments of change, believe it or not, is a specific scene from the science-fiction thriller *Prometheus* (2012).

In this scene, Dr. Elizabeth Shaw prepares herself to go into the dome to see one of the "Engineers." She has gone through a physically painful ordeal, realizes she is on her own, and is afraid. She stands in her personal quarters in front of a mirror, and sweats profusely as she swallows several painkillers for abdominal pain. As she tries to gather herself, she looks in the mirror and stutters, "Okay! Okay! Okay!" before abruptly zipping up her spacesuit over the abdominal wound. Shaw winces in pain as she zips up the spacesuit because even though it hurts, she has to keep going. I hold this scene in my mind when I am afraid to move forward, but know there is no better option than to move forward. I, too, nod my head in agreement as I stutter, "Okay! Okay! Okay!" I quickly zip up my (proverbial) spacesuit, feel the fear, and keep "putting one foot in front of the other."

How to let the universe support you:

- ○ Know you are worthy to receive all the support you need.
- ○ Look for evidence of support.
- ○ Bear witness to examples of support by sharing these experiences with a trusted friend, confidant, or family member.
- ○ Pay attention to moments of support as messages to discern a sense of direction for your life.
- ○ Remain in gratitude for *all* the ways you receive support.

3. Let the Experience Flow

When you let the experience flow, you allow yourself to be receptive to new experiences and opportunities. For example, a friend may ask you to accompany her to a luncheon. In your soul center, you may feel excitement at the idea of attending such an event, yet your response is "No." You ignore the internal prompt to say "Yes" because you worry about how you'll pay to attend the luncheon. With the lack of trust and openness coupled with fear, you mentally shut down any possibility that you can attend the luncheon, because you can't conceive of where the money will come from. When you are open to let the experience flow, you trust that you *can* be open to new experiences. Within the space of trust and openness, resources find you.

Let's be clear, I'm not talking about irresponsibly saying "yes" to any- and everything. I'm talking about times when an opportunity for an experience speaks to you and calls to you in a meaningful way. You may not completely understand why it calls to you, but later, you will. When you let the experience flow, you find a comfortable balance between focus and release, effort and effortlessness. You put forth your most sincere effort to be open and receptive, and then release your attachment to the outcome. Release of your attachment allows the love imbued within the energy of your "yes," to let the experience be what it is meant to be.

How to let the experience flow:

○ Be open to new opportunities to create the way for expansion.

○ Keep your body relaxed, light, and receptive.

○ Focus your highest intentions and actions on what you want to attain, achieve, or create, and let intuition move you into the expansion of right response.

○ Remain in awareness that the qualities of abundance, faith, curiosity, and brilliance can only flow through you if you remain open and receptive.

○ Remember, you do not know all the possibilities that can emerge within a situation or what is available for you.

○ Trust and release your attachment to an outcome.

4. Create the Pathway for Expansion

Expansion calls for you to make a conscious decision to allow yourself to expand. Your body, being, and mind want to expand, but this cannot happen unless you create a pathway for expansion. The stripping away of false identity and thought patterns, along with the release of attachment to limiting stories, possibilities, and beliefs, allows for expansion to begin.

For a variety of reasons, your mind is accustomed to believe in few options for what is real and what is possible. The possibilities that you know of are limited, when compared to the vastness of possibilities available to each and every one of us. Expansion calls for breaking away from limited thinking and limited possibilities. You will have to recondition your mind to see beyond what is in front of you, so your imagination can believe in what is beyond you. What is vital to understand is that your expansion rests upon two very important factors: *what you can imagine* and *what you can believe*.

5. Maintain a State of Calm

As far as being calm throughout change, well, sometimes you won't feel calm. You might need a minute to regroup, and that's okay.

You can, however, do your best to remain calm by remaining in touch with your heart, your breath, and your soul center. Allow yourself to settle into acceptance to temper a reactive mind. Again, amidst change, the discomfort will not vanish, but you will begin to see uncomfortable circumstances with fresh eyes.

Practical approach to maintain a state of calm:

- ○ Have daily quiet time to reconnect with the Presence.
- ○ Develop a habit of quietude and contemplation through meditation, prayer, reading, taking a walk, or whatever works best for you.

○ Remember, you can always breathe in and out on the
following thought:

> *"All will be well because all is well."*

6. Believe It, Then See It

"Your beliefs about yourself are reflected in the outer world, in your
relationships, in your circumstances, and in events in your life, which
mirror your beliefs about yourself. Our beliefs shape our perception of
the world, but they also shape our knowing of the world. They actually
structure the connections between neurons in our brains that allow us
only to see who or what we believe in. So, when people say, "Seeing is
believing," it's actually the other way around. Believing is seeing."

—Deepak Chopra

You can see the life you want to create for yourself, and for others, without
knowing how it will come about. As you strengthen your belief in unseen
possibilities, you make the shift from what "I can't" do to what "I can" do. This is
one of the most important actions you will take. The power of belief cannot be
overstated as you reach for new possibilities.

CHAPTER FOUR

HIDING THE HARDSHIP

"When you are feeling irritated, annoyed, or angry with someone, or with their choices, know that the situation is 'great medicine' for you. There is a tremendous benefit demonstrating something that needs to be revealed about you, not about the other person."
—Dr. Sue Morter

For two and a half weeks we have a family member stay with us who is visiting Los Angeles. To be clear, I am not aware we will have a houseguest because Dennis (conveniently) does not mention it until the last minute. It isn't until he opens the front door to walk out to go to the airport that he thinks I should know. I sit on the sofa in my "poor me"/sometimes meditation spot, watching TV at a reasonable volume, while he stands at the front door to put on his shoes. Leaving shoes at the front door is one thing we both still agree on.

He bends down to tie his shoe laces. "I'm going to the airport."

I ask, "Why? Who's coming in?"

"My cousin."

"Oh. She's visiting again?"

"Yeah."

"Who will she stay with this time?"

"I told her she could stay here."

"Oh. How long will she be here?"

"I don't know. Maybe six months."

"Um, what?"

"I think she'll be here for a few months this time."

"Did you tell her she could stay with us for six months?!"

Awkward/angry silence.

"I'd better go."

I don't know how Dennis arrived at the conclusion that this would be the best way to approach this situation, but nevertheless, he did. There is *no way* we will have a house guest for six months! There is no way we can accommodate her and the baby, with five people in a two-bedroom, one-bath living situation. What the hell?! This isn't the first time his cousin has come for a visit. She visited during the previous summer for two weeks, when we first moved into the apartment after losing the house. However, it wasn't a problem at all. Since it was summer, the kids were at my parents' house for weeks at a time. So when she and the baby were here, space was not an issue. But with it now being fall, the kids are home, are in school, and sleep in one room with two full-size beds and Gavin's toddler bed. With his cousin and the baby here, they will have to sleep on one of the kids' full-size beds. That means Greyson and Mckenna will have to share a bed, and five people will sleep in one room, not to mention that our kids will have to be extra-quiet in the room while the baby sleeps. It may sound petty, but I know it will be a problem. Six months is out of the question for our environment. Now, if we had a larger house, where she and the baby could have their own private room, it wouldn't be an issue, well, at least not as big an issue.

When you have infrequent visitors for short periods of time, it's easy to hide embarrassing personal circumstances. But when you have people stay with you, those embarrassing circumstances are exposed. Problems are visible. What if the gas company representative makes another unexpected visit while they're here? What if the power is shut off? What if she notices the lack of food in the refrigerator, or the ongoing tension between Dennis and me? I can't have that!

I am a person who values privacy, and I safeguard my space. It's not that I don't want to have any visitors, but neither Dennis nor his cousin are specific as to how long the visit will last. The majority of Dennis' family reside in another country. When his family members visit the States, it is not uncommon that visits are long-term, and range from a few weeks to several months. Usually arrangements are made beforehand for them to stay with a family member who has the space to accommodate the long-term visit. We do not have that space. So when I finally ask his cousin how long the visit will last, and am told "probably" six months, I am beside myself. Although, to be fair, I don't believe the entire six-month visit will be with us, but I want to be clear that anything longer than a few days will be too much. I have too much to hide to have someone observe our life for a few weeks, let alone six months! Two days after she arrives, as we lie in bed before going to sleep, I quietly tell Dennis, "You have two weeks to deal with this. And if you don't, I will."

Throughout the entire visit, I am uncomfortable with someone else being in our home. It is not that I don't like his cousin. Her presence taps into my concerns of our destitution being on display. It's one thing to deal with hardship behind closed doors. It's an entirely different thing to have all you prefer to remain hidden out on full display. I do not want anyone to know how broke we are, how difficult it has been to feed our family while Dennis takes what he can find for work, and look for work. Dennis still works in the home improvement and construction sector, and has not held a significant job for almost three months. He picks up work here and there, but money is beyond tight. It is practically nonexistent. I want to continue to deal with this privately, but when his cousin arrives, the situation quickly escalates.

She and I are not in personality agreement with each other. I am viewed with disdain by her for the empty refrigerator shelves, the disconnected cable box that sits beneath the TV, my rudeness, and the lack of money to purchase home essentials like dishwashing liquid and laundry detergent. The display of lack and poverty that occurs on my watch is looked at with disdain because I am the educated one, and educated people don't have difficulty finding jobs. I equally view her with disdain over some of her parenting decisions. As if I have everything figured out, I sit in judgment of the way the formula for the baby is prepared in a plastic bottle and then placed in the microwave to heat, how she stays out late into the night and once rings our doorbell at 2:00 a.m. because she doesn't have a key, then later decides to take Dennis' house key off his key chain without telling him…so she won't have to ring the doorbell at 2:00 a.m.! There is a certain way to be a guest in someone's home, to conduct yourself, manage your child, and be respectful of the adults in the house. I do not want her to get too comfortable, so I don't make an effort to be accommodating. I am not the welcoming host one would normally expect; in fact, sometimes I am downright mean. For example, one afternoon I vacuum when I *know* she is trying to take a nap with the baby. I could have left the bedroom door closed to only vacuum the hallway. Instead, I open the bedroom door and make sure I thoroughly vacuum underneath the

beds, the train table, and the throw rug. E–v–e–r–y single time she cooks and
leaves dishes in the sink for more than an hour, I complain to Dennis when he
gets home. If I come home in the afternoon, after running errands, and find
her sitting in the living room with the blinds drawn watching a DVD, I don't ask
one single question or say anything to her. I swiftly open the blinds and say, "I
like light during the day," and walk out of the living room. As the days pass, I
make less eye contact and less conversation, as does she.

I have a private nightmare to protect. I want her gone so I can go back
to being a private victim of my circumstances, and feeling bad about my life
without having it on display. By the end of the second week, the situation can
no longer be contained. It is ready to burst, and it does.

One morning, as the kids and I prepare to leave for school, I go outside
to start the car. We are having problems with the car battery and I want to make
sure the car will start. I put the key into the ignition, turn it, and hear "click,
click, click." The battery is dead, again. "Damn." I look at the cars passing by on
the street. 'I'm going to have to ask her if I can borrow her cell phone to call
Dennis to come back home to jump-start the car." With stifling irritation, I get
out of the car and walk back toward our apartment. When I open the front door,
she is standing in the hallway, in front of Greyson and Mckenna, yelling, "These
are the rudest kids I have ever seen!" My eyes widen in shock. I quickly walk
over to the kids and stand between her and them. She and I are face to face
and of equal height. I look directly at her and sternly say, "Calm down, Rachel!
What is going on?!" She yells, "I have never in my life seen such rude and
disrespectful children! Kids would never act like this in my house!" Greyson
has been known to make comments, or speak his mind out loud as children
often do, by asking questions like, "How long are they going to be here? Who
keeps using all the toilet tissue?" Throughout her stay, Greyson's questions
imply he has her and the baby in mind whenever he asks something I hope
she doesn't overhear, but suspect she does. Apparently, this morning, she has
had enough. So have I.

With her baby lying on the bed, Gavin still asleep in our bed, and
Greyson and Mckenna standing beside me, looking horrified, she and I go
beyond insulting each other. We scream profanities at each other and make

hostile threats while our children hear e–v–e–r–y single word and watch in complete shock. Any momentary hope I have of keeping our argument quiet so the neighbors won't hear is completely "out the window." We are so loud, and I am so pissed! I am mad at her, at myself, at Dennis, and the entire damn situation, and I do not hold back my words, nor does she. Dennis doesn't know what's going on until his cousin calls him on the phone. She yells into the phone for him to get back home before she "kicks my ass." Knowing he can hear me, I yell in the background, "I'm not scared of you," and also demand he get home ASAP! By the time Dennis arrives, I am following her around as she storms from room to room, getting the baby dressed and packing their belongings. She packs all the food she has in our refrigerator while yelling that we will starve without her food. While stuffing their clothes into the suitcases, she calls her mother, uncle, cousin, and friends to tell them all about my bitch-like tendencies. I simply cannot believe I am having this experience. It is surreal.

I always thought I was "above" such repugnant behavior, but apparently I am not. I feel justified in my anger and my need to cover up what I want to remain hidden. I want to defend myself, to defend the foolishness of my behavior. This is not all my fault! Well, maybe it is. At the end of the argument, and end of the day, our house guests are gone, and my secret is out. By now, after the string of heated phone calls to family members and the two friends who showed up to pick her and the baby up, their entire family must know about our argument and our situation. I embarrassed myself. In a very messy way, I reacted in an aggressive and inflammatory way by projecting my fear-based issues onto her presence in our home. Apparently, I haven't made as much progress as I thought.

This is a quintessential example of what can happen when pain, fear, unresolved angry emotions, and irrationally perceived threat play a role in reactionary decision-making. My emotional pain and shame were front and center, and in complete control of my destructive thoughts and behavior. But, to be fair, Dennis should not have handled the situation as he did. He should have talked with me when she asked if they could stay with us. Again, he is angry with me, and our communications are not the best. Also, I'm sure he doesn't want to say no to his family. He wants to be in a position to host his family members. I understand why he wants to do that, but this is not the way to handle it. His passive-aggressive way of handling the situation contributed to my fear of exposure, as well as the anger I felt towards everything, including him. And, as on many other occasions, I lashed out in a reactionary and self-sabotaging way. First-hand experience reiterates my knowing that emotional reactions based in fear and anger often cause more problems. This time is no different. It is clear, I have a lot of inner work to do.

For the next several days, the tension at home is thick. Dennis does not speak to me, nor I to him. I have not sat in meditation since his cousin left. The internal agitation has eased since his cousin's departure, but I am by no means in a good place. It is time to resume meditation.

It is another quiet morning, with nothing out of the usual, and the kids are at school. This time I sit on a new spot on the floor in front of the sofa. The bottom front of the sofa serves as my makeshift "pillow" for back support. As soon as I close my eyes, "HELP!" jolts through my mind like a runaway train. It is hard to concentrate this morning. I sit for what feels like an eternity trying to slow my thoughts. "I am so lame! Nobody understands! What am I going to feed the kids for dinner? Is that a bill collector I hear outside walking towards our door? HELP!" I continue to take deep breaths until, finally, the thoughts slow. I take even deeper breaths and exhale more slowly. The silence slowly filters out the mental chatter. A few more breaths and there is space to call for guidance.

"I call upon my Higher Self to join me in my meditation. During this meditation, I ask that you protect me from any and all vibrations, energies, frequencies, and communications in all directions of time, past, present, and future, that are not of love, light, and the highest good. Today I ask for assistance to gain clarity on how I can begin to release the anger. Please let this communication be clear. Let the answers be communicated to me in a way that is easy for me to understand. Please let me feel your loving energy when you are ready to begin. I thank you in advance for your presence." Luckily, it didn't take as long for guidance to drift in as it did to quiet my mind.

This is the guidance that comes through:

Nothing is futile. *Everything happens for a reason. Every time you feel discomfort, it is clarified even further what you seek to do, be or have. Nothing is futile; not even the "unbelievable" experiences (argument with houseguest). Nothing is a waste of time or energy. For, in every single interaction, an impact has been made on some level, be it advisory, influential, a connection, or a fleeting pleasantry, no experience is futile. Embrace it all, irritation and joy, because at the end of it all there is a better understanding of who you are, what needs to be healed, celebrated, or dissolved. So pay attention to what is at hand because it is never a waste of time in any sense.*

Importance of being grounded. *We love your commitment to growth. We love that you are understanding the relevance of being centered and grounded. It is comparable to being in a firmly built house in the midst of a downpour. The outside is soaked, but the inside remains untouched. Ground yourself when you are in the storm, no matter how laborious it may feel. Ground yourself to keep your love intact. The more grounded you are, the more easily you will be able to withstand the "storms" in life. Silence yourself. Go within and feel the wholeness of who you are…unharmed, unscathed and steady. THIS is you, not random chaos. You are steady. You are steady wholeness, steady strength, and steady calm. You can always come HERE and pull all scattered parts of yourself back together. Take your time. It's a steady journey, not a competitive race.*

Everything is rising to the surface. *All that you have been concerned about (mainly financial) is rising to the surface to be dealt with. It has come to the surface as a result of prolonged thinking thoughts like, "What if we can't pay this? What are we going to do?" You are not at the point of experiencing the prolonged questions because your questions consistently anticipated lack. You are in a different space and time now. The feeling, attention, and thought process is VITAL. You think about it, and it basically appears. You are here to, among many lessons, master your energy, how you use it, and how your energy affects others. You have created a world where people are severely limited (or so it is perceived) without financial resources. These past few months have shown you that, even amidst the most dire financial circumstances, there are parts of you that remain intact and will always remain intact because no material possessions can touch the deepest parts of your core Self. Your life must be initiated, energized, and experienced from the core Self, deep within your heart, where love resides. You experience lack and limitation when you live and operate from your topical, surface body/mind, when your life is based upon your outer experiences. Pull from deep within yourself the inner knowing that NO MATTER WHAT is encountered, it is minimal, and you remain intact as a being of love.*

When painful and fearful thoughts are dissolved, everything else will fill the space within you, and THAT will be what was originally present, what is rightfully present, and what is graciously present...your love body. It wants to expand, just as fear did, and it will expand because there is now a universal presence birthing itself in your world that will unconditionally support the nourishment of love presence instead of fear. You feel it happening because so many of you have willed it to be so. So many have longed for harmony, a loving humanity, nourishment on all levels, peace, and calm. The collective wanting of this was once scattered and fragmented. Now it is collectively uniting and creating the energetic pathway on a macro level (and micro!) for this to come to pass. This transition required powerful souls to weather it. This is why you are here. You are anchoring the new. What will you choose for your planet, your world, your life? This is your time to choose and create, choose and create...choose and consciously create.

Speak from your heart. *Lastly, no matter how difficult you may feel it is, find the words to say what is in your heart. Speak from your heart to your husband, your children, your parents, your friends, to yourself and those you do not know. Speak from your heart through your actions, through service to others, through your writing, and through your energy field. Let your heart serve as your compass for where you need to go, what you need to do, and how you need to be. There is no better way to live than to lead a life that is directed solely by your heart and all its good will. Within your heart, there is no room for worry, doubt, or shortcomings. There is only space for love. The love within you is seeking to express itself, which is why you always intuitively know what to do. Let love lead you because it will not lead you astray. You may not understand the path of your heart, but it is always leading with, through, and for love. Let it be.*

SUMMARY

Nothing is Futile

When a crisis or tragedy occurs with you, a family member, or loved one, you immediately go to a thought process about what is happening. You think you know what to think or believe; therefore, you think you know how to interpret what is happening. This is not to say that terrible, uncomfortable, or unwanted things do not happen. Yes, all sorts of things do happen. We often have experiences that we wish had not come to us. And there are experiences which, at the time of occurrence and thereafter, are simply too painful to process or be with. Such experiences and events are extremely difficult to view through the lens of "everything happens for a reason." When you experience difficulty, betrayal, or even hardship, how can you take a statement that says, "Everything happens for a reason" into your heart and hold it as you go through such painful times? How do you carry such a statement when some experiences in life are difficult and painful beyond imagination? The statement "everything happens for a reason" is by no means to imply that you should be dismissive of what happens, or stifle your feelings. "Everything happens for a reason" suggests an option for you to be willing to hold the perspective that you do not know what all the possibilities are for a given situation or experience. From a limited perspective, there is a tendency to label something that happens as either good or bad, or to believe it can only be what you think it is, and nothing else. On a higher level, you could not possibly know the significance of all that is happening as a result of a crisis or difficult experience. What if there is something beneficial or purposeful within the crisis, that is beyond what you can see from where you are? When you are willing to invite a more expansive perspective, you can then hold the questions which ask, "Could there be more to this? Is there another way to perceive this?" Sometimes the answer will be no. Sometimes you may be in so much pain, or discomfort, that there simply is no way for you to perceive the experience to be anything other than what you currently perceive it to be. But, at a different time, the answer will be yes. You will be able to look at the situation through a wider lens to extract something. What that something is is for you to determine.

Key points to remember:

○ Everything happens for a reason, including the reasons you are not yet able to fathom or to perceive.

○ Experiences and interactions (joyful and unpleasant) serve to provide a better understanding of where you are in your growth process. They bring your attention to the following aspects of yourself:

1. What is surfacing to be healed (restored to wholeness)

2. What can be celebrated (honored)

3. What is to be dissolved (disintegrated)

○ For every single interaction, an impact has been made on at least one of the following levels:

1. Advisory (Note: *What do I need to know? What subliminal information can I derive from this interaction and/or experience? What is the significance of what is being relayed to me in this moment? How does the information "speak" to my soul center?*)

2. Influential (Note: *A meaningful impression, thought, feeling, or interpretation occurs.*)

3. Connection (Note: *A relevant association is made between a person, thing, idea, event, intuitive thought, experience, etc.*)

4. Fleeting Pleasantry (Note: *Afterward, you may say, "Well, now, that was a nice experience," "I'm glad I saw her," "I'm happy I attended the event," or "That was so much fun!"*)

Practical approach: This is a simple yet expansive approach you can use when you find yourself in a difficult situation, such as when you are afraid to move forward, take action, speak up, interact with someone, say what is on your mind, make a telephone call, or do something you want to do but feel fear, apprehension, or hesitation about:

To quell the hesitation, moments before you take action you feel compelled to take, stop for a brief moment to imagine this subtle whisper in your ear:

> *"I do not know what all the*
> *possibilities are."*

2. The Importance of Being Grounded

> *"And once the storm is over, you won't*
> *remember how you made it through,*
> *how you survived. You won't even be*
> *sure whether the storm is really over. But*
> *one thing that is certain, when you come*
> *out of the storm, you won't be the same*
> *person who walked in. That's what the*
> *storm is about."*
> —Haruki Murakami, Kafka on the Shore

When I began to write about the importance of being grounded, I was prepared to write that I consider myself a grounded individual by virtue of being calm. However, being calm and being grounded are two completely different things. To be calm simply means to not be agitated. Well, I was relatively calm during Rachel's visit, at least up until the argument. My interaction with Rachel revealed that I was wrought with fear and overreaction, and equally overwhelmed; thus, as in this situation and many others, I did not behave as if I felt safe and protected, because I didn't feel safe and protected. I was mentally and emotionally "all over the place," dependent on the external factor of money as a determinant of my safety, security, and sense of ease. This is not to say that money does not provide a form of safety and security. Of course it does, but money should not be *the* determining factor in whether I feel safe. That is not the responsibility of money. That is my responsibility.

When you are grounded, you feel the pull of the connection that bridges your physical body with your spiritual body; you have awareness within your body. You have a sense that energy flows within and through you. It means you feel energy in your body because YOU are in your body. When you are grounded, you are in alignment with your center (your core Self), the fundamental parts of yourself, and the spiritual heart of the universe, because you are connected with the earth. The cultivation of inner alignment provides an inherent response and ability to find safety and trust within. Here, in the state of being grounded, you stand in a more solidified position to offer stable responses, in lieu of agitated reactions, no matter what is going on around you. And the more grounded you are, the more easily you will be able to withstand the "storms" in life.

When you are not grounded, you may feel mentally, emotionally, and even physically scattered, "all over the place," as if you are unable to consistently act with composure, level-headedness, and ease. You may not feel safe or protected, or you may feel irritated, on edge, or anxious, like I did. When something goes wrong, your mind will immediately want to "run like a startled horse" you cannot control. Living in the world and having so many varied experiences can leave you feeling beaten up, like you have been pulled around by life's "reins". It can be hard to believe that you can feel safe without an external intervention or "savior." However, you can have a sense of safety and security in being grounded, which can be strengthened through meditation. The reaction that I was not safe, and that there was something to be feared due to money problems, was not real. Yes, you read that correctly; not real. On the surface level, it looks like it is about money. But, beyond having your basic needs met, it is not solely about money. It is about the examination of deep-seated emotions and beliefs which influence us. It is about underlying emotional pain, emotional wounds, formulated core beliefs as a result of painful experiences, and how this combination expresses itself in your life. Although I was calm within my crisis,

I was far from being grounded. This emotionally unhealthy combination was a foundation to create and react to my own self-perpetuated "storm."

During a storm (*crisis*), the trees outside are cold, wet, and blown about by rain and heavy gusts of winds. Leaves are blown off the trees (*you*), some branches bend and some snap (*emotional reactions*), but the roots remain firmly planted and untouched. The tree roots (*consciousness*) absorb the rainwater from the soil, while also taking nutrients (*useful information*) and chemicals (*personal interactions*) from the soil (*environment*) and using them to produce what is needed for the tree's growth, development, and repair. Deeply grounded, the roots anchor the tree in the soil, keeping it alive as a steady presence within the storm.

When a storm arises, it is our relationship to the energy of the storm that determines whether we suffer or not. You can absolutely change your mind about how you choose to go through the storm, specifically a storm you may have created. It is not just about being like a tree and standing up straight amidst the storm. The storm is not there to teach you how to remain straight, which is precisely why the storm can be useful. It is there to teach you how to bend, when to yield—how to meet adversity with strength and flexibility. When you recognize misplaced emotional reactions, you can connect with what is true. A sense of safety and protection is cultivated within *you* because you begin to trust in a deeper part of yourself. At some point, we all face storms. The question then becomes: When a storm arises, can you remain centered and connected? In essence, can you remain still? Can you find the gift you can use for growth?

3. Everything is Rising to the Surface

According to Eckhart Tolle, a highly revered spiritual teacher and author of one of my favorite books, *A New Earth: Awakening to Your Life's Purpose*, "There is such a thing as old emotional pain living inside you." Unfortunately, many of us, if not all of us, to some degree or another, have residual emotional pain living inside of us. One reason the emotional residue of painful experiences lingers within us is that the body remembers emotional pain. You can test this out by simply thinking of a painful personal experience, such as abuse, loss through divorce, heartbreak, the breakup of a relationship or death of a loved one, self-betrayal, or the betrayal of others. When you recall painful experiences, if the emotions around the experience have not been processed and released, your body can feel as if you are in the moment of that experience all over again. Over time, the painful experiences can accumulate to lead to major life crises, as emotional residue can express itself as guilt, shame, fear, anger, distrust, resentment, unhealthy relationship attachments, lack of ambition, or even financial failures. When we think of emotional pain, and the emotional residue as a result of the pain, we tend to associate it with big things, like tragedies. However, emotional pain is not always the result of something big. Painful experiences can also stem from little things, like criticism, defeat, having a more intelligent and successful sibling, seeing how our parents handled money, our relationships, and the ways we communicated with our friends as children. Over the course of life, we have tons of painful life experiences that, when we do not fully face them, end up coloring our impressions of ourselves. And it is both big and little things that sink down to strengthen and grow our core beliefs, and over time can lead to a collective representation of pain known as the "painbody."

Tolle explains the painbody "…as an accumulation of painful life experience that was not fully faced and accepted in the moment it arose. It leaves behind an energy form of emotional pain. It comes together with other energy forms from other instances, and so after some years you have a "painbody," an energy entity consisting of old emotion. It shifts from dormant to active when something triggers a very strong emotional reaction. Everything it says is deeply colored by the old, painful emotion of the painbody. Every interpretation, everything it says, every judgment about your life, about other people, about a situation you are in, will be totally distorted by the old emotional pain."

Despite the recognition that I felt extremely uncomfortable with the potential exposure Rachel's presence represented, not once during her stay did I stop to further examine what lies beneath my fear of exposure. Instead, I let fear and emotional pain take the lead in determining my actions. It determined my course of action and continued to encourage negative thoughts. My fear-based reaction to Rachel's presence, and what it represented, intensified with each passing day she remained in our home. The fear of having our hardship revealed felt equatable to death, and, as you see, I could not let that happen. I could *not* let myself "die."

At the time, my resistance to being "discovered" appeared to be the easier reaction than having to honestly face the core of the problem. Simply put, I was not ready to acknowledge the shame and embarrassment I felt. No one, I thought, who is as smart and capable as I was assumed to be, could ever end up like this. If I were smart and capable, I would have never lost a house to foreclosure; I would have never made decisions that contributed to financial devastation, marital discord, and career stagnation. No one was supposed to know that, despite a degree in psychology, neatly articulated sentences, and a firm handshake, underneath it all, there was more to my story.

Everyone has what are referred to as core beliefs, which operate in the background, on an unconscious level. The core belief is fundamentally the strongest belief you hold about yourself, or about something. It can play a vital role in reactionary decision-making, and is the primary belief that additional negative beliefs use as a springboard to build upon.

The unconscious negative core belief can often be the driving force of fear-based reactions, thoughts, and perceptions. This was blatantly evident in my reaction to Rachel's presence in our home. Her presence served as the external stimulus which triggered the resistance and fear associated with the negative core belief, and my painbody.

Unconscious emotional pain creates circumstances that will allow it to rise to the surface, to the front and center of your life. These circumstances arise and serve to bring your awareness to parts of yourself that can be healed. I now understand my limited interpretation of the conditions and circumstances have little, if anything, to do with being smart and capable. It is about underlying emotional pain, emotional wounds, formulated core beliefs as a result of painful experiences, and the fact that this combination can only be suppressed for so long.

Until you are willing to be honest about yourself, underlying emotional pain, and the presence of a negative core belief, the underlying emotional pain will continue to show itself through unwanted circumstances, interactions, and experiences. Sometimes we can't know who we are until we realize who we are not. It requires raw and sincere willingness to really look at the parts of ourselves that we would rather not see, or let others see. In other words, a large part of this is about you and your willingness to be honest about yourself. When you become aware of what operates in the background on an unconscious level, you can use the awareness of the emotional pain to establish direction for your healing. Holding onto shame, fear, embarrassment, anger, or whatever it may be that lingers within you, is precisely what keeps you anchored to the situation or circumstance you want to be free of. However, it is important to note, when you look at a situation or circumstances through the filter of irrational and self-imposed defensive behavior, that unwanted circumstances can appear as if something is happening *to you*. Through the aforementioned filter, such irrational and defensive behavior can appear rational. With identification of the self-sabotaging patterns you have forged as a result of the negative core belief, you bring the unconscious belief to the surface to consciously acknowledge it, and ultimately to let it go.

"I'm not good enough", is what I tried so hard to hide, not only from Dennis' cousin but also from myself. "I'm not good enough" is the core belief I validated every time something went drastically wrong. And "I'm not good enough" was the underpinning of all I was able to see when I looked at the financial conditions of my life and began to fully acknowledge what I had let them become.

As a result of the argument with Rachel, the opportunity arose for me to dig as deeply as I could, on my own, without a therapist, to try to understand why and how I allowed myself to behave as I did.

I recalled an exercise from one of the books I had read, in which you ask introspective questions, and continue to follow the answer up with "why" to help you recognize the core of the problem, or in this case, belief. I didn't do this exercise exactly as I remember, but I do recall the emphasis being placed on the intent to uncover the core belief. By utilizing the fundamental intent of this exercise, I was able to gauge recognition of the core belief by comparing it to previous uncomfortable and revealing conversations (sometimes arguments) I've had with Dennis. I know when he says something about me that is true, or at least something I believe to be true about myself, because I simply stop talking. I stop arguing and I get quiet. The body knows truth, and you know when something said strikes a "chord" of truth. How do you know? In my case, the impetus to deny the truth was not present because I was ready to be with what was now at my "surface."

One afternoon, a few days after Dennis' cousin left, I walked through the apartment to make sure Dennis had not made an unannounced afternoon trip home to pick up more tools. Sometimes he comes in and I don't hear the front door open. When I was sure I was home alone and could speak candidly, I went into the bathroom and shut the door. I sat down on the edge of the bathtub and literally held the following conversation out loud with myself:

Question to self: What am I trying to hide?

Answer from self: The fact that we don't have any money.

Question to self: Is that all? There has to be something else. Be honest. Is that all?

Answer from self: No.

Question to self: What am I *really* trying to hide?

Answer from self: Shame.

Question to self: Shame about what?

Answer from self: I feel ashamed of myself.

Question to self: Why?

Answer from self: I lost our house to foreclosure, I don't have a job, and it's not supposed to be like this!

Question to self: Okay, those are experiences. *Why* do you feel ashamed of yourself? Be honest!

Answer from self: Because I feel so stupid. I've embarrassed myself, my family, and I've made mistakes. *That* means I am a failure, and *that* means I am not good enough.

Question to self: This feels familiar. Have I ever felt shame like this before?

Answer from self: (*Sigh*) Yes.

This shameful feeling *is* familiar to me. I felt this way sometimes as a child when I was criticized. Somewhere along the way, during the experiences of criticism, I must have internalized the criticism and concluded (formed the core belief) "I am not good enough."

I have noticed it is extremely painful for me to feel the feelings associated with making a mistake, or to listen to someone tell me I've done something wrong. I don't want to be criticized because I don't want to feel ashamed or embarrassed. It hurts too much.

(*Sigh*) Oh. So that's what this is about.

This situation completely mirrors some unsettling emotional experiences I periodically felt as a child.

Until you sit and thoroughly consider your core beliefs, and why you have these beliefs, they will look indistinguishable from reality. The belief in my own unworthiness most likely expressed itself in a million little ways over the course of the years. However, from my unexamined perspective, it did not look like an expression of beliefs. Instead, it looked like…life.

For example, for the period of time with financial setback after setback, I began to tell myself I did not have any control over the situation. I began to tell myself that this is simply what life is, a series of financial setbacks and unfair shortcomings. I then began to formulate all kinds of mental rules and hidden tests that a situation of financial lack must perpetuate and validate, like "money is short-lived," "my bank account is always empty," or "we'll never get ahead.." Instead of being able to relax when I had money, I became cautious, and even more worried. Having a little bit of money left me more afraid of running out of money, rather than being able to accept and enjoy the fact that I actually had money! Without ever examining where the distrust of not having enough and being enough derived from, I could have carried on like this for decades. I could have continued to believe that this is the only way life shows up; therefore, it must be a characteristic of life itself, not the way I see, interpret, and respond to life.

When you become aware of the belief, awareness moves it out of your subconscious to the surface to get your attention. The surface, where you are conscious of the belief, is the only place where a belief can consciously be healed. The only way a belief can be changed is if you change it on a conscious level.

Examples of negative core beliefs:

- I am a victim
- No one ever listens to me
- If I show vulnerability, I will get hurt
- No one loves me enough to do that…
- Illness is the only way for me to get loving attention
- It is not safe to show affection because I will be rejected
- People I depend on abandon me
- People I love disappoint me
- I have to suffer to earn money
- I will never live the life I really want to live
- I am not smart
- My efforts are not acknowledged
- Everyone loves my brother/sister more than me
- Success is for other people, not me

○ I am not good enough

Here are **contemplative questions** you can use to further clarify the negative core belief of "I am not good enough" (for example):

○ What do I believe about me, or my life, is not good enough?

○ Why do I believe this?

○ What have I done that, I believe, makes me not good enough?

○ How do I determine what "good enough" is, or what it looks like in the world?

○ Am I aware of how I reinforce this negative belief?

○ As a result of my reinforcement, how does the experience of this belief show up in my life?

4. Speak from Your Heart

The enormity of the financial pressure took a toll on me. I grew tired of trying to avoid and delay uncomfortable conversations. Although it had taken some time, I began to grasp that one of the most important things you can ever do for yourself, and others, is to speak from your heart. I am not talking about speaking in a sappy or "syrupy" type of way that can be insulting and annoying, nor am I talking about revealing too much private information, leaving you feeling invaded and vulnerable. What I am talking about is being honest about what you really want to say, and really want to do, by inserting sincerity into a conversation where it may not be present. I am talking about speaking with words and action to honor the person with whom you speak, as well as yourself; speaking with the intent to get to the truth of the matter without manipulation and coercion; and speaking from your heart with conscious presence that is authentic, unassuming, and yet empowering.

Before I came to grasp the importance of verbal authenticity, over the years, I initiated and participated in conversations that were nothing but clever semantic attempts to evade, manipulate, or control an outcome. It was exhausting, and frankly, afterwards, I didn't feel that great about myself. I knew what I was doing. I know that, in certain instances, I've spoken in a manner I consider to be verbally superficial.

For the most part, it is rather easy to speak from the heart when I talk with my children, a beloved family member, my best friends, and—during non-stressful times—my husband. But when I consider a conversation with our landlord, a bill collector, and sometimes myself, there may be discomfort. However, there can also be a major shift. For example, some time ago, my daughter received a substantial scholarship to attend a two-week summer art camp. The tuition was not completely funded by the scholarship, and I was asked to contribute $300 to pay the remainder of the balance. Again, for some, $300 is change, but, for me, it was a lot. I agreed to pay the $300 and was grateful that it was a nominal amount. Although I had a few months to pay the balance in full, due to deciding what to pay immediately and what could wait, I repeatedly put off making the summer-camp payment. Finally, after receiving a series of monthly reminder invoices, one week before the start of camp, I received an email and two voicemail messages from the Accounting Office Assistant requesting that the balance be paid in full. Immediately. Two days after receiving the email and voicemail messages, I had not replied because I didn't have the $300. The following morning I received a third email from the Accounting Office Manager with a stronger and more direct tone. The email read:

Mrs. Jackson-Buckley,

We will charge the card we have on file tomorrow morning at 9:00 a.m.

Thank you,
Mrs. Dodson

Up until this point, the communication between me and the camp accounting officials was succinct and cordial. Now, by my own hand, I was dealing with yet another awkward financial situation. I was so embarrassed. Before I responded to Mrs. Dodson's email, I thought long and hard about my reply. I had grown of tired of my willingness to make up extreme excuses and participate in avoidance. I was no longer interested in making a dishonest statement on my behalf. This time I would not concoct some kind of personal crisis to blame for stopping me from making the payment. It was time to put on my "big girl" pants and just deal with it honestly. I took a few deep breaths, sat down in front of my computer, and typed the following email:

Mrs. Dodson:

Regarding the balance for the account, I received the email message from the Office Assistant, as well as two voicemail messages. Please know I am deeply embarrassed, and it is not my intention to ignore you. The reason I did not respond isn't because I am trying not to pay the balance. I did not respond because I do not have the $300. As soon as I can pay the balance, I will.

In gratitude,
Bridgitte

No drawn-out, lengthy sob story or pity party, just the plain truth. Ten minutes after I hit SEND, Mrs. Dodson emailed the following response:

Mrs. Jackson-Buckley,

Thank you for letting me know what's going on. I completely understand when the expenses surpass what is available to pay them. Please don't be embarrassed. I've been there.

I've attached the registration pass and room assignment for Mckenna. Please give me a call when you are ready to pay the balance.

Sincerely,
Mrs. Dodson

It is amazing how unwieldy something can become when we refuse to face it. Of course, the above example is not an exact approach to every situation. However, what can be an exact approach is the intention with which I began the communication–to be honest without attachment to the outcome. I had no idea how Mrs. Dodson would respond, nor did I send the email with an idea of how I preferred that she respond. However, as human beings, we know what other humans are going through, and Mrs. Dodson willingly acknowledged this with her response. Of course I wanted Mckenna to attend camp, but I also knew I would feel so much better about myself if I at least took a step toward authenticity, instead of more inauthenticity. Yes, I could have avoided the situation, as most of us usually can. However, we're ready when we're ready, and nothing will change until you change.

Surprisingly, speaking from the heart in a straightforward and intentional manner is refreshing, not because the outcome yields what you want, but because it affords an opportunity for you to sincerely face what needs to be faced, no matter how uncomfortable and awkward. It is a reclamation of power when you understand it is a situation and not aspect of your character. Empowered individuals can acknowledge a circumstance without allowing the circumstance to define them or their character.

A few days later, when we arrived to drop Mckenna off at camp, I was able to interact with Mrs. Dodson and the Office Assistant without avoiding eye contact or feeling ashamed for not having been truthful. I was able to walk through the situation knowing that, even though the balance remained, all was well. In fact, the balance was paid in full before Mckenna returned from camp.

CHAPTER FIVE
LETTING GO

Since Dennis' cousin left, almost three weeks ago, I continue to go through a series of emotional ups and downs, moving in and out of worry and calm, wondering why I still have the urge to volunteer and what we will do about food. It is amazingly awful to live in one of the most prosperous states in the nation and deal with food insecurity. Day in and day out, the kids have to eat. We have to eat. Every day I drive past grocery stores filled with aisles of food. It is difficult to grasp how hunger can be an issue in this day and age, especially with the resources and technology available. Walking into the kitchen knowing there is no reason to open to the refrigerator is dismal torture. Empty refrigerator shelves can't keep secrets. They tell everything. The emptiness brazenly speaks for itself to tell stories of poverty, malnutrition, something unattended to, financial shortcomings, evasive conversations, and failed attempts.

In the weeks following Rachel's abrupt departure, we are down to one half-gallon of milk, water, three Hebrew National hotdogs, two wheat buns, powdered sugar, and a half-box of pancake mix in our refrigerator. Despite the fact that I wanted her gone, I miss opening the refrigerator and actually seeing food on the shelves, even if it isn't our food. It was a temporary, but welcome, relief from emptiness. And now here we are again. Empty. With no end in sight. Something has to be done, and I know what that something is, but I do not want to do it. Dennis alluded to it on maybe two occasions prior to this in heated arguments. I'm not sure if he brought it up out of desperation, in anger and wanting to throw something in my face, because he doesn't know what else to do, or all of the above. The two times the subject came up, my ego quickly reminded me I am a Spanish-speaking UC Berkeley graduate and defiantly dismissed the suggestion. Of course, Dennis doesn't really want to go that route. Who does? He wants me to get a job, and he wants consistent, well-paying work. Even though I think of it as the last of the last resort, have I exhausted every possible option? Well, not really. I have not applied for work in fast-food restaurants, or to clean homes, but I am still applying for work below my educational level with no responses or offers on the table. Have *we* exhausted every option? Is Dennis working hard enough? Absolutely. There are qualities about Dennis which I can definitely say are irritating. However, lack of work ethic is not one of them. If there is ever a person who works until he drops from effort and exhaustion, it's Dennis. His work ethic far surpasses mine and rivals only that of my stepfather. If hard work were all that is needed to do well in life and be financially prosperous, Dennis would be a millionaire by now. Throughout these years of the economic recovery, Dennis has been working more for less money. And no, it is not just my imagination. With the rise in the cost of living and higher food prices, the money doesn't go as far. If this continues, we will be on the brink of starvation while I go through the routine of looking, applying, waiting, hoping, for work. Something has to be done, something has to give.

On Monday morning, after dropping the kids at school, I drive to the local public library. I will sit in the car and wait for over an hour for the library to open. I don't mind. I will use the time to think, to find another reason, other than downright embarrassment, not to go through with it. However, as much as I want that to be enough, embarrassment is not enough to sustain us. We need food, not here and there, but e–v–e–r–y single day. In the stillness of the empty parking lot, amidst the growls of my reluctant and empty stomach, I make a decision. Tomorrow morning I will go to the Department of Social Services to apply for food stamps.

On Tuesday morning, a non-preschool day, Gavin and I sit in the car waiting for the left-turn light to signal green. To my left, the discreet building stands tall. There is no exterior sign or name on the outside of the building, only the numeric address. If you are going there, you know where you are going. Everyone else does not need to know. The light signals green, I make the left turn, immediately merge into another left lane, and stop. Again, I look to my left to see a small parking lot in the underground garage. While I wait for oncoming traffic to pass, I look at the pedestrians on the sidewalk, hoping not to see a familiar face. The building is not far from the kids' school, and although they attend school in a high socioeconomic area, anything is possible. Anyone could be here. After all, I'm here! I quickly look for my sunglasses and make the left turn down into the garage. The garage is dark, unclear, with limited parking, and one way in and one way out. It is close to 8:30 a.m. Am I early? Too late? "Please let me find a spot down here. I do not want to walk into this building from the street side." I find a spot and park. I grab my purse, open the back passenger door to unbuckle Gavin from his car seat, and close the car door with a nervous breath. Here we go. A family appears from around a corner and I ask if there is an elevator. We step inside the elevator and press one. My heart pounds. "I cannot believe I am here." When the elevator doors open, I cautiously step out, while looking to see what I can figure out on my own. A security guard notices us and points to the security checkpoint. There is a long line beside the checkpoint. I feel eyes on us as we walk by the line because (1) we are obvious newcomers, and (2) there is nothing else to look at but signs on the wall. With a quick glance up, I notice the words "Report Welfare Fraud" and something about jail time on one of the signs. I don't look directly at anyone who stands in line. I am determined not to make eye contact unless absolutely necessary. At the checkpoint, I place my purse, belt, and jewelry on the conveyor belt and walk through the security gate with Gavin in my arms. No alarm. "Is this your first time here?" The guard asks. Am I that obvious? "Yes," I say. The guard nonchalantly looks toward the people in the security line but points behind him, toward the information and check-in line. I get in line, put Gavin down so I can straighten my clothes, put my belt back on, and wait. I count the backs of twelve heads in line in front of us. Hopefully, we can make it through this without a meltdown from Gavin. While waiting in line, I notice more people coming in from the elevator and street entrance. Both the information and security lines and the murmur of voices grow by the minute. People who enter the building and join the lines are not solely the infamous "welfare queens and kings" and homeless people portrayed in the news cycle. These are people who resemble my parents' suburban neighbors, senior citizens with an adult child leading the way, young and older men in Army fatigue jackets or US veteran hats, some middle-aged women with very nice purses, homeless people with swollen legs and limps, women wearing hijabs, brown and white parents with toddlers, men speaking foreign languages I cannot place, some ghetto-ish girls and me…all representatives of the melting pot. I am shocked, still embarrassed, but shocked. There are no smiles, no jovial conversations, and no expressions of wanting to be in this building. People look for direction, read the papers in hand, pass through security, complain to the information desk clerks, and hurry to pick up or drop off paperwork, all without smiles. In the lobby, despite the flurry of activity, the energy is heavy. With an overlay of seriousness to contend with, there is no time for small talk, pleasantries, or idle conversations. After thirty minutes of standing in line, I

am next at the information and check-in counter. "Next," the clerk behind the
desk calls out. I walk forward with Gavin on my hip. "I'd like to apply for food
stamps." She asks, "Is this your first time?" "Yes," I respond. "Go into that room,"
she points to the door behind us, "and get in the line to begin the application
process." "Okay, thank you." She is polite. We follow her directions and walk
into a room with at least seventy-five people sitting in the waiting area. It's
9:00 a.m.! What are all these people doing here? I look for the food stamps
line and, surprisingly, there isn't anyone in the line. The male clerk hands me
the application, which consists of five double-sided pages asking the same
question in a hundred different ways: Do you have any money?

I turn in the forms and am instructed to go up to the third floor to wait
for a caseworker to be assigned to my case and call my name. Is that it? By
9:30 a.m. we get off the elevator onto the third floor. Every seat in the waiting
area is taken. Up here, the ventilation is poor and the energy is even heavier.
Intertwined within the rows and columns of chairs, a baby cries, cell phone
music is playing, shoes sprawl out into the aisle from people sitting against the
wall, someone is snoring, and there is *another* long line. I'm not sure what the
line is for and I don't ask. I have to find a seat. My eyes quickly glance around
the room looking for a blue opening. Anywhere. One blue chair will do because
Gavin can sit on my lap. We don't need to get comfortable. As I stand at the
side of the room looking for a seat, a woman opens the door, calls out a name,
and escorts two applicants behind the closed door. I quickly move to claim one
of the seats. An older man, who looks tired and in need of a long soak, claims
the other. Women and men open the door periodically, call names, and verify
information. Are they caseworkers? This goes on for hours while Gavin sits
on my lap, playing with the iPod Touch (supplied by Granny), and I avoid eye
contact. All I want is to hear my name called so we can get out of here.

Almost four hours later, Gavin and I still sit in the waiting area! My
name has not been called. The iPod battery is dead, he is hungry and getting
fidgety, and so am I. I finally get the nerve to get out of my seat to ask what is
taking so long. There is no line, but I wait to be acknowledged. The clerk behind
the desk motions for me to come forward. "Hi. I've been sitting here for almost
four hours and my name hasn't been called." "Did you check in?" She asks.

"No," I respond. "I didn't know I was supposed to. The man downstairs told me to come upstairs to the third floor and wait for a caseworker to call my name." "Honey," she said, "you are supposed to let us know you are here. I need to see your ID to check you in and let the caseworker know you're actually on the third floor." "What? Why do I have to let you know I'm here if I am told to come up here?" I ask. Her facial expression softens. She calmly responds, "Sometimes people leave." Without trying to hide my state of confusion, I am unsure of how to interpret her comment. Is this a sign I *should* leave? Am I making a mistake? Is this something I'll later regret? She must recognize a familiar expression of doubt on my face and quickly says, "It's almost lunchtime. Please have a seat while I let them know what's going on." Gavin squirms in my arms as I carry him back to the waiting area to find another seat. It is easy this time. Most of the people who were there when we arrived have gone. I sit down, put Gavin back onto my lap, and wonder if I should leave. "Even if I start work at McDonald's *today*," I thought, "it will be at least two weeks before I receive a paycheck." Two weeks is a long time to sit with emptiness. When you're hungry, you can't think beyond the hunger because it's always there, demanding a response, gnawing at your attention and pulling you away from the normal routine of things. A few moments later, "Jackson-Buckley," the caseworker calls out. Hearing my name jolts my attention back into the waiting area. I stand up and pick up Gavin. Why do I still carry this child? The caseworker pleasantly introduces herself and ushers us behind the closed door. We pass rows of barren cubicles. With dire and pained facial expressions, other women and men tell their stories to caseworkers. And now it's my turn. We arrive at the empty cubicle and sit down. The caseworker pulls out a stack of papers and additional forms to be filled out. The pile is comparable to a twenty-five-page spiral notebook. There are more questions to be answered. She looks at the computer screen and begins a barrage of questions: Do you work? Are you looking for work? How many children do you have? How old are the children? Are you pregnant? Are you married? Does he live in the home? Is he the father of your three children? Does he work? How often does he get paid? Do you own property? A car? Cars? How do you pay rent? Eat? Pay the utility bills? Have you won the lotto? Do you have a retirement account? She goes on and on, not in a hostile or judgmental way, but in an ask-the-same-question-a-hundred-different-ways way, to find-out the most important information: Do you have any money? I had already said "no" on five different forms downstairs. Is she double-checking my answers against tone and body language? She turns away from the computer screen toward me, leans back in her chair, looks directly into my eyes, and asks, "So what's going on?" Shame ascends and fills my eyes with tears just enough to make its presence known. I can't recall anything that has chiseled away at my ego more than poverty. I tell her how long I have been looking for work and that I cannot understand why I don't have a job. I tell her of the humiliation I feel when I repeatedly submit my resume to online job openings, only to receive no response. I tell her how hard Dennis works, but it's just not enough. I tell her how my marriage is barely a marriage because financial strain permeates every aspect of our relationship. I tell her how disappointed I am in myself. And with overwhelming deflation, I lean back in the chair, tell her I never thought I would find myself in this position, and exhale. "Okay," she says, "Do you have any food in the house now?" "No," I respond. "Well, we can help. You qualify for emergency food assistance and Medi-Cal." Health Coverage? You mean we can all go to the doctor, not just the kids?! "Seeing that you're married, your husband's signature is required on the forms as well." The caseworker hands me the stack of paperwork to return within three days. I will need to submit a copy of the rental agreement, a copy of the last rent check given to the landlord, gas/utility/phone bills, car registration, immunization and school attendance records for the kids, bank account numbers…everything. The emergency assistance will offer relief, but it also comes with the ambivalence of full disclosure and a self-imposed stigma of "welfare recipient." "You can go downstairs to the Cashier's Office for your debit card." "That's discreet," I thought. "You mean I can get the card today, with money pre-loaded onto it to purchase food?" "Yes," she says, and smiles. Her smile is the first of the day. Although she offers reassurance about the debit card, I'm nervous. That sounds too good to be true. By now it's after 2:00 p.m. I have to pick up Greyson and Mckenna, which means I do not have time to stand in another line. I will have to leave and come back. She hands me the pile of forms, offers a second smile of reassurance, and walks us to the door. She is polite and kind, not at all what I expected.

After picking up the kids, we return to the DPSS building. The crowd has thinned out. We go into the cashier's waiting room and I instruct the three of them to sit down and not say a word. Before I can finish demanding silence, Greyson blurts out, "What is this place?" I respond, "I have to pick up something. Sit quietly with Gavin and Mckenna, and don't get up!" I walk to the window. The clerk looks up my new case number and hands me a State of California Electronic Benefits Transfer (EBT) debit card. "Choose a pin number and you're all set." "Thank you. Thank you so very much."

Two hours later in the grocery store, I timidly push the shopping cart toward the checkout counters. I surreptitiously study the cashiers in an attempt to gauge which cashier will be least judgmental when I select "Food EBT" as my form of payment. How can I preserve dignity as a recipient of food stamps? Is it even possible? The reiterated message that is embedded within our society is that we have failed in a terrible way if we ever need assistance. Throughout the day, I was keenly afraid of the judgment I would encounter from the DPSS clerks, the caseworker, and the grocery-store cashier. However, my experience was quite the opposite. The negative meaning I attached to seeking food assistance sustained my belief in a story of failure, and because of this, I didn't need to look outside of myself for judgment because it didn't come from any of the people I encountered. The harshest judgment came from me and my view of myself.

Later that night, filled with remorse and gratitude, I sit on the bed with my legs crossed and a pillow behind my lower back. Despite the emotional toll of today's events, I am still in awe of the calming power of sustained silence. In a meditative position, with my eyes closed, I gently say, "I call upon my Higher Self to join me in my meditation. During this meditation, I ask that you protect me from any and all vibrations, energies, frequencies, and communications in all directions of time, past, present, and future, that are not of love, light, and the highest good. Please let this communication be clear. Let the answers be communicated to me in a way that is easy for me to understand. Please let me feel your loving energy when you are ready to begin. I thank you in advance for your presence."

This is the guidance that comes through:

You cannot escape what needs to be resolved. *We feel that you have an overwhelming desire to leave, as in run and hide. We know it is difficult. We know the lessons are sometimes very difficult and seemingly prolonged, but know they are necessary. And they will follow you wherever you are because they will remain a part of you until you recognize, heal, and release them. There simply is no other way. You have been hurt, but this hurt is not who you are. It is a brief experience you had that you have decided is more important than it really should be. Lessons should incite introspection, self-reflection, soul healing, and soul transformation, not lifelong pain and identification with pain. Your life circumstances continue to reflect what you are carrying around deep within you; a belief that something or someone left you when you most needed them. They, however, did not leave you. They chose to leave a situation. The situation did not equal you. You believed it did. You are at an energetic impasse where you must release this belief, or it will consume all your life experiences from this point on. You will feel nothing more than loss if you do not release this belief. Yes. How? Believe in where you are, right where you are. For it is from this place of being grounded that you are nourishing the growth for your next place. Be where you are.*

For the past few weeks, along with hearing the small voice within say, "You should write," I have had a strong urge to volunteer. With so many concerns around food, housing, and work, I have not posted an article on Examiner in months. Now that the emptiness is gone, I can think again. As a returned Peace Corps volunteer and occasional volunteer at the kids' elementary school, I wholeheartedly believe in volunteering. The benefits of altruism, possibilities, and good will that come with doing something you do not have to do are far-reaching. However, in my current situation, this makes absolutely no sense. Why would I volunteer when I have no income? To volunteer now is the antithesis of being responsible. It could not have come at a worse time. I don't want to have to explain the decision to volunteer to Dennis or to my parents. I'm not interested in having one more conversation when Dennis looks at me with the "*I'm trying to understand how, and when, you became so misguided and out of touch*" look, or my parents' attempt to understand "*where we went wrong.*"

For several months now, I have consistently checked the Employment Opportunities online section of the spiritual center for a position to which I can apply. I periodically attended service at the center over the years, but after giving birth to Gavin, I didn't consistently attend service. During his toddler years, he didn't want to be left in the childcare center. He was too rambunctious to remain quiet during meditation. It wasn't until he was a little older that I could attend service on a more regular basis. "Coincidentally," when we lost the house, the first and only tenant application I submitted was for an apartment literally three minutes from the center. By coincidence, or divine placement, the proximity to the center, along with Gavin being older and now enjoying the children's center, is the perfect outcome. We can attend on a regular basis and be a part of a supportive community. A five-minute drive from the kids' schools and in alignment with personal growth that interests me, the center is the perfect place to embed myself within an organization that contributes to a rise in consciousness by way of helping people. This is what I have been looking for all along, to do work for the greater good, beyond the financial bottom line. The problem is that the organization rarely has job openings. I have checked the website consistently for months. I mailed in an antiquated paper copy of my resume so it would be on file in the event of an opening, and even called the receptionist's desk to see if an opening was available that was not yet posted on the website. Nothing. Are there no openings because staff members are so happy working there they never leave? I can't think of a more perfect setup for a work situation than this, yet I have an unfounded urge to volunteer that will not go away.

One week after consistently opening the refrigerator to fullness, I stand at the kitchen sink washing breakfast dishes while Gavin sleeps late. The notion to volunteer continues to prompt me with unfounded persistence. "Since I'm not sure what this urge is about, or what it signifies, maybe I should meditate on it instead of continuing to be dismissive," I thought. By giving the logical mind a rest, meditation helps me get out of my own way to get a different perspective. Sometimes it is not clear what the best route to take is. Aside from the possibility that volunteering can be a way into the organization, we just can't afford this now. I dry my hands on the dish towel and walk to the living room. I sit on the floor with my back against the front of the sofa. I have not sat in meditation for two days. My body feels as though something vital is missing. I want to detach from knowing how to proceed.

The warm light passes through the blinds to ease the firmness of the floor. Sunlight hits the bottom of my legs and welcomes stillness. It is difficult to meditate without interruption with Gavin at home. I will sit for as long as I can while he sleeps. I breathe slowly to sink into relaxation, lose track of time, and pass into being. I take several deep breaths, settle into gratitude as the words "Thank you," float into my awareness. I am grateful the emptiness is gone. I say a prayer of gratitude for known and unknown ways grace is available to me and my family.

"I call upon my Higher Self to join me in my meditation. During this meditation, I ask that you protect me from any and all vibrations, energies, frequencies, and communications in all directions of time, past, present, and future, that are not of love, light, and the highest good. Please let this communication be clear. Let the answers be communicated to me in a way that is easy for me to understand. Please let me feel your loving energy when you are ready to begin. I thank you in advance for your presence."

This is the guidance that comes through:

<u>Allow your Higher Self to reconnect with your worldly self.</u>
We can understand why you are hovering in fear, but we do not recommend it. When you dwell in a state of fear, nothing can get through. Nothing. We are here. We move with you, amongst you, beside you. We whisper to you. We inspire feelings. We communicate, but only some of the time do you hear. You have felt the prompts, you recognize the deep inner knowing, you read the transcripts, but you still doubt. You question the validity, and you question if the message is really for you. It always is. The message is always for you. We communicate with you in all manners, through numbers, feelings, nudges, resonances, and readings. We are sending messages of remembrance on a daily basis to you. Continue to move in alignment with your intuitive prompts. Do not be doubtful about you. We know that in the three-dimensional world there is very little validation of what is felt, what is known. It is difficult sometimes to separate influence of the ego, fear, needs, and wants from that of inner knowing. You wonder, where does inner knowing stem from? Is it subconscious influence, the Higher Presence, you, or resistance? You know when it's YOU. You can feel it. But what happens is, the subtlety of the message is contaminated with fear and doubt. This is the challenge. This is the crux of the experience. Your Higher Self is trying to emerge. It wants to live through you, but the world you have created makes that very difficult; not impossible, but very difficult. All that resonates within you is an attempt of your Higher Self to reconnect with your worldly self. It is a reminder of what lies beneath. You know who you are. You know who you want to be. Allow the connection of the two. Allow the reconnection.

Move toward growth, toward the life force. *You know that there is a purpose to all, that there is something to be done, something to be fulfilled. You are well beyond feeling this to be true. You know this to be true. You are on your path, not with unwavering faith, but you are on your path. Every experience you have can lead you closer to, or farther away from, your purpose. You feel this every moment of your day with small choices that lead your life circumstances. The choices either resonate high or low (vibration) and you are able to feel life growing, or shrinking, within you. When you feel growth, love, excitement, and energetic surge, you know you are moving toward your path and are planting your feet firmly onto your path. Your strengths, your interests, your small but heartfelt encouraging moments, are moving you to love in your purpose. And know that you are doing your part of what needs to be done. Do it well and do it to be of service to others. We know that you are unable to see all that needs to be seen that would give you comfort and hope; but because you cannot see it, you must believe it to be possible. You must first feel that it is possible. You must feel the life into vision. You must create. Feel it until you see it. Remember this when times are uncertain. Remember to move toward growth and toward the life force.*

The pull of old and destructive patterns. *Simple things should not pull you back into old destructive patterns. Fear. You are afraid of the outcome of a few things now. Very simple things that are pulling you back into old destructive patterns. Shield yourself. Let love flow through you. As more love flows, the fear subsides. You are well. You remain well. But you must believe this to be true.*

You have questions about career and other things. You are being moved toward that which you seek. When your choice feels haphazard, quick, and reactive, this is fear. When the choice feels as if it is a comfortable, relaxing perfect fit for where you are right now, you are being led to love. Move toward love. You know that which you seek. Look for it. Expect it. Ask for it. Talk about it. Expect miracles. Align yourself with that which you seek. Know it is your time. Honor your clarity. Embrace where you are…this stepping stone into the NEW. Walk forward and know you are never walking alone. Love.

<u>Let love express itself in, around and through you.</u> *Even during your deepest, darkest moment of fear and doubt, we remained. We hovered near you extending love to you. We love you. You are reaching for more love in your life. Good. You have felt closed off, alone, and sometimes misunderstood. You have tried to "protect" yourself from "hurt." But now you are beginning to see that the only way to truly protect yourself is to let love express itself in, around and through you. Love brings you alive. Love softens you. Love moves energy. We will continue to encourage you to feel into existence all that you seek, as its beginning is always within and through love. Love of yourself. Love of life. Love of knowing. You are love and we love you. Love is where you are. Let it be.*

I open my eyes to Gavin climbing onto my lap. "Good morning, love," I plant a kiss on his cheek. "We have to get you fed and dressed. I have an errand to run."

Gavin plays in the children's section of the Los Angeles Public Library while I connect my USB drive to the computer. Maybe the rigid expectation of how I think a job should enter my life is keeping me stuck. Maybe it is time to stop wishing and hoping things were different, and instead look more closely at what is in front of me. Guidance makes itself readily available to me in many ways, but especially through meditation and intuition. When will I be willing to truly listen and consistently let go? Fear has held me back from doing a lot of things I have wanted to do, and on too many occasions I let fear close my mind to possibilities. Maybe, just maybe, this is an unconventional opportunity to move into a different experience of perception. Instead of harboring the positions of "this isn't the right time" and "this isn't how I want it," I can settle into the idea that an internal call to volunteer represents a larger possibility than I am currently able to perceive, the opening of a new pathway. At this moment, I don't have to know what the larger possibility is, or what it will yield. My opportunity is to decide which will have the prominent role in my life, fear or courage. I pause momentarily to check for the sunken feeling I normally have when I apply for jobs I don't really want. It isn't there. This is different. There is no heavy, sunken feeling in my stomach, only an unfamiliar curiosity: Is this how higher possibilities attempt to meet us where we are? At our level of understanding? Through mundane intuitive prompts which arise when you least expect them? Fear tries to prevent me from trying something different, something new, despite the outer circumstances which beckon for a new approach.

I locate the contact information for the volunteer listings in the center's email newsletter. I read over the position description, type a brief introductory email, attach my resume, sink deeper into uncharted territory, and, with resounding familiarity, hit SEND. Two days later, I am called for an interview.

SUMMARY

1. You Cannot Escape What Needs to be Resolved

In addition to going to the Department of Social Services to apply for food stamps, there were other occasions when I wanted to run and hide, and not deal with what was at hand. One of the hardest things to do is to bring hidden parts of yourself out into the light, to own what you have repressed. Crisis and challenging situations are available for you to learn from, to initiate introspection and self-reflection, to uncover hidden biases and beliefs that need to be resolved, not to render more self-judgment. What my life circumstances reflected back to me, what I could not escape, was that I carried a consciousness of poverty. As much as I wanted something other than financial crisis, I placed most of my attention on what was missing from my life instead of looking at what was trying to enter. I was heavily attached to the way I thought something should enter and how it should be made available to me. I had come to expect financial obstacles, problems, and more setbacks. Where did this come from? In part, this came from me not wanting to be disappointed, not wanting to be too hopeful, and not wanting to expect something that may not show up. The Notice to Quit, house foreclosure, and food stamps are physical representations of scarcity, loss, relinquishment, wanting what is not present, absence, in other words, representations of unresolved subconscious issues around abandonment. I would not be able to escape what needs to be resolved because wherever I go, there I am. If I wanted to break the cycle of suffering, I would have to release the wounded parts of myself that were entrenched in abandonment, and process the shame and self-judgment I inflicted upon myself. Shame reinforces the cycle of poverty consciousness. If I didn't release the parts of my consciousness that are rooted in shame and abandonment, whatever came into my life that represented prosperity would not have enough grounding to stay. It would be fleeting because a consciousness of poverty, loss, and shame only allows more of the same.

Practical approach to release what no longer has a place in your life:

1. Recognize that it no longer holds a place in your life, your thoughts, and your expectations. (*Feelings are emotional responses to meanings. I choose to recognize the feeling of abandonment is one of loss and that I am owed something. I can release the feeling of being owed something. I can recognize that the feeling of abandonment no longer has a role in my life to cause anything other than harmful feelings.*)

2. Let it flow out of you. Breathe in love, breathe out loss and abandonment, and remind yourself you have released it.

3. Believe in receiving. Believe in worthiness. Believe you are enough. (*Begin to look for ways I am now being loved, and be gracious for loved directed to me.*)

4. Feel the life that is now able to move through you, as a result of releasing lack and abandonment. (*Begin to believe I deserve good in my life.*)

5. Forgive. (*Forgive the person who I associate with abandonment, with negative feelings.*)

6. Now forgive yourself.

2. Allow Your Higher Self to Reconnect with Your Worldly Self

During the week of applying for food stamps and the volunteer position, I dreamt a statue of an angel appeared in our apartment. The statue stood tall against the dining-room wall, and was made of stone, resembling a gray granite cemetery monument. I was terrified of the angel, and scared to go near the statue, but there was no way to avoid it. In an attempt to get out of the apartment, I ran past the statue. Just as I passed in front of the statue, the head moved! In the dream, my heart pounded as the angel's head followed my movements and the eyes stared at me. I ran out of the apartment in hysterical fear and stopped at the neighbor's door. I pounded on the door to be let inside, but sensed something behind me. I hesitantly turned around, and there, standing behind me, was the statue of the angel. The angel peered at me with a perplexed expression. She was trying to figure out why I was so afraid.

During the process of socialization, as you are groomed to fit into society, you can become heavily attached to identities associated with the worldly self, and out of touch with the Higher Self. You can be distracted, withdrawn from practices and beliefs that don't fit your curated view of the world. You can become attached to mental habits that lead you to routinely misinterpret experiences in your life. And, to your own detriment, you can be dismissive of your own inner resources, afraid to get in touch with a deeper part of yourself. As a deeply complex being, you have at your disposal a vast range of inner resources. These resources, such as intuition, imagination, heart intelligence, resilience, the power of the mind and the world you build in your mind, consciousness, courage, the soul, and the Higher Self, speak in ways you can understand, but there has to be willingness to act. It is easier to recite guidance that comes through, or even read a book on spiritual practice, than to *act* upon guidance. Change seldom comes easily, and will require a significant amount of courage to stretch yourself and act from the direction of higher inner resources, especially when it fails to make sense to the logical mind. This is not to say guidance consistently goes against logic, because there can be cohesion. The logical mind has a role, but so does the heart, in creating the balance to allow your Higher Self to reconnect with your worldly self. Imbued with sincerity, consistency, accountability, and clarity, this connection can be a powerful inner resource available to help guide you, to move you toward less separation and less fear, and toward the highest course of action.

3. Move Toward Growth, Toward the Life Force

To move toward growth is a call to find the courage to let go of doubt and the "what-ifs" that stop you from experiencing a new aspect of yourself and of your life. It is to first recognize that movement begins with small everyday choices.

These small choices present themselves at every moment of the day:

○ Will I choose to ignore this phone call, or answer it and deal with what is at hand?

○ Will I choose to help my children with their homework or watch television?

○ Will I choose to continue to believe in my dream, or will I let it quietly fall away because it's just too hard?

○ Will I choose to trust and believe in myself, when others will not?

○ Will I choose to be compassionate and caring, or remain judgmental?

When we move into a place of consciously considering what it is that we would like to create, we start making choices from a place of empowerment that asks:

○ Does my choice support love, well-being, integrity, and sincerity for others and myself?

○ Does my choice connect with my intuition?

○ Does this choice maintain consistency between my actions and my beliefs?

○ Does this choice help me to do what I say and to say what I mean?

During the moment of having to make an important decision for yourself, or on behalf of someone you love, is the time when you are able to see yourself at your best or your worst. Small, everyday moments offer the choice of character development, the opportunity to center yourself in conscious decision-making, which leads to a feeling of empowerment as you move towards growth. We can choose responsible attitudes and behaviors that we want to implement in our lives, just as we can take actions and make choices that are rooted in truth—our own truth—when what we say, what we do, and what we believe are in complete harmony. We can simply make the choice to make better choices, choices that in some way or another support personal wellness, because ultimately, each choice affects whether you move toward wellness, or away from wellness—where you are no longer making choices to avoid something, but instead are making choices to create something.

4. The Pull of Old and Destructive Patterns

In retrospect, I had to let go of the parts of myself which blocked conscious decision-making and forward movement. The resistance to letting go of wounded aspects of myself played a part in keeping the refrigerator empty. For example, in order to apply for food stamps and for the volunteer position, I had to begin to let go of identities associated with who I thought I was supposed to be. I was not supposed to be a food-stamp recipient. I was not supposed to experience lack of response to my resume. And I surely was not supposed to be in a volunteer position at this age. Or was I? There was something in me that knew I had to volunteer, even if I didn't fully understand why. On the surface level, it appeared as merely being prompted to volunteer. On a higher, more expansive level, I was prompted to have trust in the inner knowing that was introducing a new way of being in the world and new form of self-trust. The fact that the intuitive prompt to volunteer spoke so loudly suggests that—on a higher, more expansive level—it had already connected with the larger possibility. I just had to get out of the way and have trust to take the encouraged action. If I wanted to move into a higher experience of myself and life, I would have to learn to be emotionally and spiritually nimble; to not be lulled back into old patterns of fear and distrust. I would also have to let go of inhibiting mental habits to gain the psychological flexibility to try new approaches. Each decision, or action, offered in the intent to increasingly become a better version of yourself, helps to soften the mental rigidity which keeps you bound to old patterns, habits, and perceptions. However, you shouldn't deceive yourself by assuming the process of releasing what no longer serves you is a one-time event. It's not. It's a continual process which requires ongoing self-reflective inquiry into what needs to stay and what needs to go, and re-choosing to be better and do better. From this place of renewed clarity, you can begin to imagine, grow, and if necessary, begin again.

5. Let Love Express Itself In, Around and Through You

Khalil Gibran wrote in *The Prophet*, "All these things shall love do unto you that you may know the secrets of your heart, and in that knowledge become a fragment of life's heart." Without the expression of love, life force is stifled. The experience of giving and receiving love wisens us because we cannot have what we are not willing to become. In giving love to ourselves and others, the presence of love carries the vibration of transformation. It draws out our highest and best qualities, and encourages us to express ourselves into maturity, to allow the very expression we came here to experience and share. When we experience and share love, the energy of the heart is protected from stagnation, from slow disintegration. Love is the most powerful human emotion we can have, yet many associate love with pain and vulnerability and go to great lengths to block the full experience of love. Like personal growth and change, love can be a process by which we experience new ways of giving and receiving love, as we drop the guard around our heart. If we would just be willing, even in momentary increments, to *feel* what is in front of us, there is no way our experience of the beauty of life will not be transformed by love—and by the heart.

CHAPTER SIX

THE ROLE OF FAMILY IN SPIRITUAL GROWTH

You are immersed in a specific environment, with specific individuals, conducive of self-reflection and the cultivation of inner depth through greater self-understanding.

Within these environments, with these specific individuals, you find yourself with people who each represent some aspect of yourself; therefore, the people in your life, and the environment in which you find yourself, serve as nothing less than a personalized mechanism of feedback. When you consider the people around you, it is by no means a coincidence that you find yourself in relationships that are "tailor-made" to assist in the development of personal growth based upon total honesty and humble learning. If you look closely at the individuals in your life, it is possible to recognize the complexity of divinely interwoven relationships. Take a moment to consider the people with whom you work, share a familial or social relationship, or are connected romantically. Have you ever wondered, on a fundamental, subconscious level, why these people? Why that person? Why are these individuals in my life? Why am I a part of their life? The feedback you receive from your interactions, and the ways in which you approach the people around you, is constantly revealing something to help you further develop and improve yourself. However, if you are not ready to see what your environment and the people around you reflect back to you, it will not be seen.

As human beings who are more alike than unlike, you are parents, friends, siblings, uncles, aunts, co-workers, grandparents, spousal partners, nieces, and nephews, who are "mirrors" of each other. The primary purpose of a mirror is to reflect. The mirror is there for you to look at what is reflected back to you. When you look at your reflection in a mirror, the reflection beckons you to open your eyes to look deeply to see your true reflection—to identify what is not real, what is not truly you, so *you* can let it go. The reflective mirror also applies to the people in your life. When you experience these individuals as "mirrors" —the reflections of yourself in another person—they reflect the virtues and qualities you admire in yourself, as well as the shortcomings and qualities you reject. What you see outside of yourself and dislike, in someone else is an aspect of yourself which you have not embraced within yourself. The same applies to what you see in someone else that you like or admire. It is an aspect of yourself which you *have* embraced. The people in your life also reflect your deepest beliefs, even the beliefs you did not choose. We all have aspects of ourselves that we want to hide from, be separate from, reject, and avoid. These aspects are easy to identify because you judge them and attach negative labels to them. You may label some people as lazy, controlling, demanding, moody, emotionally unavailable, shameful, or too aggressive, to name a few. You may label without hesitation to examine where, when, how, and to whom you may exhibit the exact same qualities and behaviors. The people around you are there to show you which qualities to hold onto and which qualities to let go. Their presence in your life can also bring to your attention the importance of not pushing away what is there to embrace. In their own way, each person is in your life to help you remember who you are, just as you do the same for them.

Contemplative Questions:

1. "Which qualities can I embrace from my family?"
2. "Which qualities from my family can I let go?"

It is the desire and willingness to learn from the people around you that creates the experience for learning. However, due to the possibility of a flawed perspective created by lack of objectivity, there is a caveat. When you look at the "mirrors" in your life, you can choose to see only what you want to see. It is only when you sincerely make an effort to see yourself reflected back that you come to understand there is no need to take anything personally, dole out blame, sit in judgment, or render yourself a victim, because when you are ready to see, you will see. Keep in mind, you are human, and there may be occasions when you do take something personally, dole out blame, or sit eagerly in judgment. However, you can still take steps, no matter how tiny, to transform the relationship with the energy and the individual.

While employed on the research project at USC, it was a pleasant work experience. I worked with a small group of people who were all efficient, professional, and interested in doing good work of integrity. We all got along well. There were no major relational problems, office feuds, or anything of that sort. However, there was one coworker who served as the project and budgetary supervisor on the secondary project which corresponded with our main project. At the time, the secondary project supervisor was a younger graduate student. As the Budget Technician for both the main and secondary projects, I worked with her for project budgetary items. For the most part, she and I got along well. When we held meetings between the two of us, we conducted business in a polite but relatively cold manner. Without having had a verbal disagreement, it was clear, on a quiet level, that there was distance between us. When she made requests, I often responded by doing only what I was asked and nothing more. During office social events, our conversations were routinely forced and guarded, and I noticed that we rarely sat at the same table for lunch.

One morning, she came into my office to go over budgetary expenses related to the secondary project. While she sat across the desk in front of me, I thought, "She bothers me. She's cold and guarded." Later that evening, while standing at the kitchen sink washing after-dinner dishes, the secondary project supervisor was still on my mind. Something about her gnawed at me. "Why does she irritate me so much? What is it about her?" I scrubbed the pan, and stood quietly with the warm water running over my hands. Out of nowhere, or perhaps from a residual self-help-book memory, a thought seeped through. I looked up and out the window, and stood completely still, staring into the backyard at nothing. "She is cold and guarded, and so am I."

For as long as I live, I will never forget the impact of that single "aha moment." The revelatory insight was astounding. She was the mirror of internal qualities I disowned and rejected within myself. The strong emotional response I felt towards her was simultaneously the trigger and the gift. My response let me know exactly what I needed to look at within myself.

From that moment on, the course of our interactions completely changed for the better. The resistant energy, which was normally present when she made a perfectly appropriate business request, lessened. Going forward, during our budgetary meetings, I was able to sit across from her at my desk and see her from a softer, non-judgmental place. I no longer held her at a distance. There was no need for emotional agitation. Once I recognized what was going on, what I projected onto our interactions, the energy around our interactions and my thoughts about her shifted. The contempt I once felt was now replaced with compassion for her and for myself.

It is from the relationships with family members, friends, colleagues, and especially those who push your emotional buttons, that you are encouraged to look at who you are so you can plant a different "seed" in your collective lineage of relationships. Relationships provide an opportunity for you to heal emotional wounds and self-negating beliefs at the level where you are, so you don't take them with you where you want to go. When you are ready, you will become aware of "teachers" and "mirrors" who show you where the next stage of healing needs to occur. There is a wide range of individuals from whom we can learn. We can learn from those who have surpassed us in age, life experience, or expertise, as well as those who are younger than us; those who embody an enlightened consciousness and are still tethered to wholeness. They are our children. *The children know and remember love, lightness and life. They have come to help you. Your role is to love them.*

I was raised with the notion that children are to be seen and not heard, which often means one does not speak until spoken to. While there is a level of respect to be upheld for adults, I have grown to recognize from first-hand experience that there is much to teach children, but also much to learn from children. With so much noise in the outer world, it is helpful to engage in some form of deep self-inquiry. Here you can revisit the wounds of unmet childhood needs and unresolved expectations. Many, to one degree or another, are dealing with childhood wounds and the way in which these wounds handicap your life. Although many of you are doing the best you can, one of the most important roles you will ever hold in this life is to preserve the wholeness of children by delving into your own fears and shortcomings, to heal your own incomplete nurturing, deep hurts and brokenness. With a rich inner landscape of love, innocence, and wonder, children also serve as mirrors. They are mirrors of our forgotten Self.

With this in mind, I consider our children, who by their very existence encourage healing and personal growth. They are reflective bellwethers of what it is to move from observation to acceptance and into the spiritual, as they reflect the subliminal stages of growth in my life. It wasn't solely the births of our children which changed the course of my life, but also what each would show me, and what I would in turn show them…letting go, turning within, and beginning again–stages of the past, present and future.

Letting Go with Greyson

Our first-born has light in his eyes. It smiles when he speaks. He is jovial and ready to bring laughter to social interactions. He is kind and physically expressive.

Throughout his infancy, toddler, and preschool years, I bought the best I could afford for him. He wore forty-dollar sweaters and sixty-dollar shoes, and was smothered with material goods and rarely told "no." Greyson was born during the time of "yes," ten years before the foreclosure, before the crisis, and before I recognized the under-developed relationship I had with giving and receiving love.

Greyson's expression of love has brought my issue of giving and receiving love to the forefront of our parent-child relationship. During his elementary years, I began to notice a feeling of slight discomfort with the extent of love he expressed towards me. He would tell me he loved me, and would often kiss me on the arm because he couldn't reach my cheek. Although this was coming from my child, it felt foreign. Greyson saw me in a completely different way than I saw myself. I was emotionally guarded, protecting myself from the vulnerability of fully showing him, in a way he understood, how much I love him. I wasn't used to expressive, unconditional love being given to me in this way. I am used to gifts, time, and material comforts, not this. It was hard to accept. And sometimes, to my own detriment and his, I pushed it away.

One morning, when Greyson was a little older, we sat in the living room waiting for an Uber driver. The kids and I were going on vacation with my mother, without Dennis. While sitting on the sofa, Dennis tried to joke around with Greyson, but Greyson was monumentally uninterested. Dennis finally grabbed him in a playful manner to kiss him on the cheek. Greyson was visibly upset and extremely uncomfortable! He told his father, "Can you please just get off me?!" I watched in nothing less than horror. There was absolutely no reason for Greyson to respond in such a way. Dennis was being loving with him. I asked, "What's going on with you? Why would you respond to your dad that way?!" Greyson said, "You do the same thing! What's the difference?" I was mortified. I sat in complete silence looking at Greyson, thinking, "What have I done?"

The heartbreaking discomfort was the realization I had created the same limiting emotional environment in Greyson that I experienced as a child. I consider myself compassionate, empathetic, and capable of love. However, in my daily actions, I rarely display this side of myself. Throughout my adult life, there is a primal need to "protect myself" from being vulnerable by not showing my need to receive and give love. It's odd and backward, and ultimately a fear of intimacy, yet it's the way I have been for so long. During childhood, I must have interpreted that it is not okay to demonstrate how much you love someone through physical affection and language, and that love should be expressed by "doing." I "do" all of this for you, therefore I love you. Parenting a child as loving and physically expressive as Greyson has helped me to recognize the complexity and depth of spiritual connections, and that I have to separate my emotional past from the present. He is here, in part, to bring to my attention the importance of not pushing away what is there to embrace. It is okay. There is no need to enclose my heart. I can let go, accept, and receive love. It takes time after I witness his reaction to Dennis, but I work up the courage to have a candid heart-to-heart conversation with Greyson. It is not his fault I reject his physical affections, there is nothing wrong with him, it is all me. To the best of my ability, I explain to him that he should not allow my emotional wounds to become a part of his identity.

It is a process for both of us. Little by little, I watch his reacquaintance with loving affection. His presence, in part, serves as a reflection of what it means to let go in order to receive. I had to let go of an emotionally unhealthy part of my past to keep it out of his future as well as mine.

Turning Within with Mckenna

When I made the decision to stay home with my newborn daughter, I told myself it was because I wanted to be the primary caregiver for her, for my children. I wanted to show Mckenna and Greyson, above all else, that they are the most important parts of my life. I wanted to bond with Mckenna and provide the consistent physical presence of someone who adores her. However, despite the truth of what I told myself, there were deeper subconscious motivations. During a meditation, when I inquired about my decision to stay home with Mckenna, this is the guidance that came through:

You say, "But I have given up the working years of my life to stay home with my kids." Yes, they needed you. They still do. However, that (decision) was also for your need to work out abandonment. They (kids) never felt abandoned. You brought that into the scenario when that was your main reason for wanting to stay home. You began to live, identify, and dwell in abandonment. In that state, everything you desired of your worldly possessions began to leave you. No, you did not abandon your children. You abandoned the choice to stay home with them simply to show them how much you love them. Your choice was rooted in abandonment, and that is exactly what you have experienced... abandonment; abandonment of love, money, material possessions, perceived choice, vibrancy, and other higher vibrating energy. You, alone, created a situation of loss.

I did not fully explore what lingered beneath my unyielding position to stay home when we could not afford it, and because of this, I did not recognize the various subconscious needs underlying my decision. There were, throughout all of this, deeply wounded parts of myself guiding me in an effort to be healed.

Mckenna was born at the start of the crisis, the perfect time to anchor the presence and groundedness I would need to learn to weather my storms. Everything about her signifies an inner spiritual world that is full and nourishing, not easily swayed or pulled about. In more ways than one, her presence stirs the subliminal introduction of what I will have to learn to cultivate. However, it isn't until the middle school years that I recognize how a conditioned part of myself almost suppresses the very quality in her that seeks to emerge from me. At the start of middle school, my relationship with my daughter exemplifies the relationship I have with my creative Self. There is a power struggle present. While I attempt to make changes that appear to be beneficial to her, she stands her ground to remain as she is. She is strong-willed, tenacious, decisive about what she wants and how she wants to be in this world. With a strong sense of self, she has already determined her most comfortable way of being. In this aspect, she reminds me of how I used to be free of worry to express myself. Unfortunately, most of my negative interactions with her are a result of my attempts to get her to conform to a way of being that is of no interest to her.

When Mckenna began middle school, our morning routine was a repetitive example of the parent-child power struggle many experience. I adamantly believed it was my job to ensure that she present herself to the world in a certain way. I wanted her to wear neatly ironed, color-coordinated outfits that (I thought) made her look appropriate and presentable. Not only did she not agree, but she wanted absolutely nothing to do with an iron or *anything* that involved a coordinated fashion plan. She preferred (and still does) a consistent rotation of the same worn out t-shirts, sweat shirts, sweat pants or shorts, and flip-flops. In her opinion, the only things that matter are that she is comfortable and that *she* likes her outfit. There were several mornings when she would walk into the kitchen after getting dressed for school, when I recall looking at her with disapproval, the same disapproving look I loathed when I was her age. One morning, I recall thinking, "What will people think of me when she shows up at school with holes in her t-shirt?"

After a few months, I noticed she and I were communicating less and she appeared uncomfortable in my presence. She made less eye contact and was short with me when I asked her questions. With heartbreaking realization, I began to understand my projections of how I thought she should present herself were diminishing her sense of self. Of course, I want the best for her. It's not appropriate to leave the house looking unkempt. We know better than that; I know better than that. However, the intensity with which I demanded she dress in a certain way to uphold a certain standard had more to do with me than with her!

In the process of arguing about clothes, i.e., her self-expression, I was draining her spirit and trying to make her conform, to do as I did. I was trying to make her fit into an image that I myself didn't really want to uphold. To say the least, I was causing harm where originally there was no harm. Few experiences highlight emotional wounds more than being a parent. For instance, lack of compassion for your own areas that need growth can lead you to be overly critical and judgmental of your children, precisely the pathology I want to avoid with my children. Why did I try to make her uphold an idea I no longer believe in? Because the unembraced qualities cause us to act in disempowering ways. Secretly, I can relate to her resistance. I rarely iron my own clothes these days! There's too much to do and, frankly, I don't want to be bothered. Besides giving her the following reasons, "you want to present your best self when you leave the house," and "you want to feel proud of yourself," I never bothered to ask her if she *already* felt that way…*in* her sweats and t-shirts. Apparently, she does. Once I realized what I was projecting onto her and the problems my response caused in our relationship, I backed off and instead gave her the two following guidelines: When you walk out of this house you must be (1) odor-free and (2) without holes in your clothes. And I left it alone.

Mckenna is not here to reflect my ideals of appropriate presentation, or to serve as my vessel for public comfort. I had to decide to "pick my battles" while simultaneously giving her room to express herself accordingly. When I look at my daughter now, I think, "She is all that I want to be…again." Mckenna is comfortable how she is because she is comfortable with who she is. This is not to say there is no room for growth or self-improvement. She also has a path to walk and lessons to learn in this life. But in all that she is, right here and now, she reflects the loving self-acceptance and creative expression which is necessary to *be* in the present moment. In merely being herself, Mckenna directs me toward the inward glance, where I reflect on being who I am and where I am while allowing others do the same. In the present, with presence, I let go of thinking I know what something or someone should be.

Beginning Again with Gavin

When I started work at USC, I was almost four months pregnant with Gavin and didn't know it! To say the least, he was not expected. Gavin was born in the midst of the crisis. He was the bringer of light as our life crumbled around us.

On three different occasions, I asked our youngest son, "Why did you come to us? Why did you choose to be born? Into this family?" I intentionally asked more than once to see if his response would change or vary in any way. Each time, without hesitation, he responded, "To join in the fun!" This response perfectly captures Gavin. He is joy personified. He brings contagious energy, enthusiasm, and excitement to all in which he engages. The zest he exudes for life, and his experience as a *participant* in life, pulls at a yearning within me. His presence speaks to the longing within me for deeper engagement with life, to once again be boundless in curiosity and exploration, uncorrupted by doubt.

He often talks of wanting to travel, to go on a safari, to venture into the depths of outer space and break away from the routine of sitting in the confines of a classroom. I tell him, "I can relate, Gavin." I, too, want to go, to travel, to seek out new experiences and have the wonder for life that he exudes. Unlike a child, as Gavin has the luxury to do, I can't throw caution to the wind and be a perpetual international travel adventurer. But what I can do, what he inspires me to do, is rekindle the connection I once had with lightness, joy, curiosity, and emotional freedom. I can be an adventure unto myself.

There is a wonder to life that living as an adult makes us forget. Children help us to remember what has been forgotten. There are times when I feel overwhelmed, depressed, and filled with despair; when I want to sit in an obscure corner of my life and quietly give up. But when I look into Gavin's eyes during a difficult moment, I don't have to search for what I long to see. Joy is present. It reflects back to me as if it waits for me, inviting me to align with the joyful reflection of myself I see in him. In an effort to see truth, the opportunity lies in the honest acknowledgment of what is reflected back to you. You cannot let go of what you are not willing to acknowledge exists, nor can you grasp what is there to embrace without taking responsibility for yourself. Being truthful has to be experienced personally to be validated by you. Gavin's presence is a reminder that I do not have to approach professional endeavors, responsibilities, relationships, interactions, or even challenging situations with mental cloudiness and emotional heaviness. He is fresh, still leaning toward what can be and what is to come. He is ready to meet change, possibility, and newness with openly receptive arms. His presence reflects the light I had to find within myself to keep going forward, to move beyond dark places–to try again.

CHAPTER SEVEN

OPENING UP TO GRACE

There is no way I can tell Dennis I've accepted a volunteer position at the spiritual center. The situation between us is already fragile. Even though it's only three hours a week, I think he'll be upset. I imagine he'll say I'm "giving away" my time and effort for free, to someone else, when he needs help. I'm going to have to lie to him. I'll tell him I'm starting out doing just a few hours a week until something opens up, and that I've agreed to help with administrative work in hopes I'll find a way to do writing work at the center.

He knows I want to do more with writing, but with so many people writing online, it is a challenge to find "creative footing" to stand out. I have written several articles for Examiner, but considering the other writers on the platform, I was afraid to show myself and stayed in the safe zone. Yes, I can structure an article and demonstrate enough potential that I was brought on to write, but what terrifies me is that many online writers receive harsh feedback in the comments section. My writing is hesitant and safe, because I don't want to upset anyone. I am more concerned with what I think readers want than with clarifying what I want to say. This, I believe, is reflected in low page views.

In October 2011, after two months of volunteering, Dennis is onto me. He's noticing I'm still not paying for anything. He is realizing I lied and it's a volunteer position, and he is livid. He said he is not doing anything else to help me continue with a three-hours-a-week volunteer position that makes no difference in our lives. I am upset that he thinks he can tell me what to do!

However, when I honestly think about it, he isn't (merely) telling me what to do. There is another layer to it. He is reflecting my fear-based thoughts back to me! His reaction is an external expression of the fear I feel about doing something I'm unsure about. The logical part of me doesn't understand the intuitive prompt, and therefore, partially agrees with him, but I don't tell him that! It seems irrational to have such a strong feeling about something which does not make financial sense. I have to stay at the spiritual center. I have to find out what's at the core of this feeling, even if neither of us understands why.

One Sunday morning, after church service, on my way to pick up the kids in the Children's Church, I stop to look at the Employment Opportunities board. There is a listing for a receptionist position! I stop in my tracks and read the job description. I immediately begin to look for anyone I know at the center who can introduce me to the hiring manager or put in a good word for me. I walk anxiously back towards the sanctuary and see the gentleman with whom I volunteer. He is taken aback by my intensity when I ask if he will put in a good word for me. "Of course!" he says. "A receptionist position? I am more than qualified," I smile to myself as I briskly walk to get the kids. Since we live close to the center, I drive home, get a paper copy of the same resume I sent in to volunteer, and take it to the spiritual center to officially apply for the position. After submitting my resume, I glide throughout the remainder of my Sunday. This is it. I *know* the job is mine.

Two days later, and after having applied for at least five positions since being laid off, I receive a call to interview for a Budget Technician position at USC! And the following day, I receive a call to interview at the spiritual center. Both interviews are scheduled on the same day! Are you kidding me? I mean I'm excited, but at the same time, I can't tell if this is some kind of pivotal choice point. Maybe I'm being prompted to decide on a direction. I call my mother, tell Dennis and a few friends, who ALL agree it's a no-brainer. The hourly rate for the position at USC is twenty-one dollars. My mother says, "It's a non-profit, spiritual center. The pay will be low. I'm praying for USC." I think she is being negative, that is, until I have my interview. When the hiring manager states the ten-dollar hourly rate for the receptionist position, I gasp in shock… *during the interview.* To this day, I believe my shocked response is the reason I was not offered the job. Over the course of five days, I have three interviews for the position at USC. Ultimately it comes down to me and another candidate. According to the final interviewer, the other candidate has more accounting skills. Both positions fall through.

After roughly sixteen months of volunteering, and with no positions posted on the Employment Opportunities board, I am anxious. I am now also coming in for occasional per-diem work at the reception desk, as well as working in the Accounting department twice a week for four hours at the same hourly rate as the receptionist position. I have worked for over a year, doing my best to exhibit professional, polite, and sincere work habits to show I am worthy of employment, and what I have are four paid hours a week! One afternoon, after finishing my two-hour shift in Accounting, I knock on the office door of the same hiring manager I interviewed with for the receptionist position, to ask if I can speak privately with her. "Sure," she says. "Please come in." I close the door behind me and sit down. I am embarrassed to disclose the details of my situation, but I set my feelings aside and say what I have to say. "I'd like to talk about working in the Accounting Department. If it's possible, I really need more paid hours. We're behind on our rent and if something isn't paid soon, we'll have to move. The only place we can move to is Orange County, so I'll have to leave the spiritual center." She tells me she is sorry to hear of this, but the position in accounting is temporary and more hours cannot be approved. I stand up, say thank you, gather my belongings from my temporary desk, and leave for the day. The car battery is dead, so I walk home. After the thirty-minute walk, I open the door to our apartment, walk in, and, with a defeated slump, fall down onto the sofa. *I am done. I have nothing more to give.* "I have tried so many approaches to get hired and nothing is working. Nothing," I cry. "If I have to move back home with my parents, then fine. Fine. I can't fight this anymore. I just can't. Whatever you want me to do with my life, I'll do it…I guess from Orange County, but I'll do it. Just show me what you want me to do." I sit on the sofa for another thirty minutes, releasing with deep exhalations of surrender and tears. I have nothing left. The crisis has won.

The next morning, I arrive in Accounting for my 11:00 a.m.–1:00 p.m. shift and am met by the hiring manager. "Hi, Bridgitte. Could you please come into my office?" Oh, damn. What now? I sit down, while she closes the door and moves to sit at her desk. "I have news. Something has opened up." What does that mean, "Something has opened up"? I'm anxious to know, but hesitant to get my hopes up. My eyebrows raise, signifying interest as if to say, "Tell me more!" Yet, I say nothing. "I have a position for you. It's eighteen hours a week to work the evening security shift at the reception desk." Reception security? *That's an oxymoron*, I thought. However, yesterday, when I sat on the sofa in tears and said "Show me what to do," a deep emotional release of frustration and despair occurred, when my inner feeling was no longer tight and fearful. Unbeknownst to me, the emotional release withdrew my focus from identifying as a victim. The sincere release, coupled with willingness to surrender and let things be, initiated a powerful internal shift. And something I initially thought was a setback presents a whole new aspect of life. While it may appear that "something opening up" at the center is a random event, I *know* this is not a coincidence. Although I cannot prove it, because correlations of this type can neither be proven or disproven, the synchronicity of the job "opening" and my internal "opening" clarify that there is no division between my inner and outer world. My internal experience is fundamentally connected to my external experience of the world around me. I don't have to fight with life. And I don't have to fight with myself over what I cannot control. Yes, thank goodness, something has indeed opened up. I smile with gratitude. "I'll take it!"

After completing the remainder of my shift, I leave for the day. The thirty-minute walk home isn't the same walk as the day before. Today, it is a walking prayer of gratitude. I notice the fullness of the trees and expansiveness of the sky. For the first time in a long while, I feel free.

I arrive home, drop my bag and purse onto the dining-room table, get the pen and notebook, and sit down on the floor in front of the sofa. I sit with my heart to further receive this turning point in my life. In prayer, I graciously acknowledge the preciousness of this moment, the ways in which I am sustained, and a new understanding that spiritual insights come from paying attention to what moves me closer to wholeness. With my attention turned inward, toward Presence, my heart is light. There is "extra" space inside of me. Yes, I AM here and I am ready to listen.

"I call upon my Higher Self to join me in my meditation. During this meditation, I ask that you protect me from any and all vibrations, energies, frequencies, and communications in all directions of time, past, present, and future, that are not of love, light, and the highest good. Please let this communication be clear. Let the answers be communicated to me in a way that is easy for me to understand. Please let me feel your loving energy when you are ready to begin. I thank you in advance for your presence."

This is the guidance that comes through:

Welcome new opportunities. You are moving in the right
direction. Welcome new opportunities as they come to you,
because what you seek also seeks you. We ask that you continue
moving and walking in faith while knowing that you are well. No
matter what you perceive to be a problem or difficult situation,
come back to the all knowing that you are well.

As the intuitive prompts come to you, you must trust the prompts that you receive. You will intuitively know if what has come to you, or is being presented to you, is aligned with your intentions. This is your beginning to plant the roots of what you would like to create. Let your spiritual roots grow and flourish among the others on a similar path. Yes, it is difficult to step into the newness of who you are, but you are ready. You have tried to hold yourself back, but your purpose is stronger than your fear.

Be open to all that needs to flow through you. *Your time has come to open yourself to all that needs to flow through you. The time has come to let strength, courage, love, creativity, and the higher messages flow. You are afraid to truly stand in who you are meant to be because you think you will not know what to say and do, but you will know what to say and you will know what to do. Do not entertain worries that you may not rise to the occasion of what is being asked of you and called through you. You are here at this moment for a reason. You will grow as others will grow, you will learn as others will learn, and you will awaken as others will awaken. You will know what to do because the Presence is within you. The earth is undergoing critical, but necessary, planetary changes and as a result the entire species is being asked to change, to raise the individual and collective consciousness. The transition from a lower consciousness to a higher consciousness will be uncomfortable, but after a brief period it will then feel recognizably comfortable. These steps to move into a new way of being, you must take on your own. We cannot force you. We can only speak of the way and let you know what is happening. This great moment has been made available to you. Step into the new and embrace this moment…uncertainty and all.*

Embrace courage. *We embrace you during these times of shift and change. We embrace your courage. Know that even though you may feel alone, you are not, and you are so loved. Yes, many of you have wondered and continue to wonder (yes, you) if you are loved and are lovable. We are here to remind you that you are dearly loved. You have undertaken a massive task to be on the planet at the time of the global rise in vibration. You will rise up, but you will feel great discomfort in the midst of change. It will not feel easy. We will walk with you and help you to ease as much of the process as we can. Although you would like to, you can't make the transition easy. The time has come to let go of the old ways of being that no longer serve you. You have fearfully straddled two worlds for some time now. It is time to let go of the world of fear and move into the world of love. You feel so deeply that you want to move into faith, love, peace, and stillness, but you dwell in the fear which holds you back. You cannot have both. You are now at the time of your existence when the choice can no longer be delayed.*

We understand that for a long time you have been ruled by what you can see, touch, feel, smell, and hear. But you now sense that a much greater perception is at hand, available and within you.

You ARE where you are supposed to be. *This is nothing less than the time of trust even if it feels extremely uncertain. You have been prompted to trust in the all-knowing Presence. Love is needed. It will give you strength during this time of transition. You ARE where you are supposed to be. You asked for this experience with these people that surround you. You have been able to feel within you the deep and profound connection you have to this experience. You are growing spiritually as a result of this experience. You may feel that you are not well, but the very fact that you are now concerned with living with integrity and compassion reveals how important this has been. Honor where you are. Honor what you are. You all have different plans. You suffer when you believe you must honor someone else's plan. You are here at this precise time to fulfill what you came here to do. Do not be sidetracked. There are many disguises at play. Trust your intuition. Trust that you know who speaks of love and who is false. Go with love. Hover in love. Dwell in love. This is your salvation.*

SUMMARY

1. Welcome New Opportunities

Change in and of itself is an opportunity. It's up to you to decide how you're going to take in the change and what the opportunity is bringing to you. From the surface level of thought, I did not seek out the opportunity to volunteer. It was sought from an internal level of the heart. This is what is meant by "What you seek is also seeking you." When you sincerely reach for something better, you call resources, people, and situations into your life from an internal level. What is trying to emerge through you seeks you with as much energy as you seek it. On a heart level, the urge I experienced to volunteer required that I let go of my need to know where the urge was trying to lead me. The opportunity presented itself in a way I could immediately act upon. There is a connection between you and what is being sought, thus making it inevitable that you will meet on some level, or through some opportunity. It is in the need to know, to have certainty in the details, that I could have gotten in the way and ignored the opportunity.

Contemplative Question:

How do I get in the way of the opportunities I seek?

2. Be Open to All That Needs to Flow through You

Often I have lamented the amount of effort put toward trying to make something happen when I wanted it to happen. During such moments of doubt, I thought, "So much effort is being made, and it's just not happening." Spending vast amounts of time trying to make something happen, when I think it should happen is not flow. It is force, and in force, there is resistance. In resistance, there is none of the harmony, balance, or flow which come as a result of following the natural course of things. There is something fluid in the moment when you accept you cannot force your way to a desired outcome.

When you lighten yourself in this way, you create an opening to receive high-vibrational information and guidance to direct you in the way that is least resistant. Surrender and flow are at the heart of every personal rite of passage. It is through this that you come to understand when to act, when to remain still, and when to surrender.

3. Embrace Courage

A few years ago, I took a visioning class at the spiritual center. In the class, during the closing of one of the lectures, the instructor said, "…have the courage to follow your heart." At the time, I didn't understand why that would be important, but I never forgot it. The word courage comes from the Latin root *cor*, which means "heart." To embrace courage means to embrace living with heart. Years later, I often recall those very words which lie at the heart of all the progress I've made.

Without courage, you cannot move beyond the convenience of a comfort zone that perpetuates what you think you know. You cannot grow without the courage to do what you think is right and necessary. And without courage, you cannot let go of the mental insulation which stops you from being an adventure unto yourself. Courage insists that you compassionately draw out the best of yourself when facing challenging times. In reality, you probably don't think of yourself as courageous. I didn't either. However, each time you allow yourself to become vulnerable, share your flaws, allow yourself to shine, admit when you're wrong, speak up when you witness an injustice, establish boundaries, or refuse to hold yourself back when your intuition says to move forward, you *are* being courageous. Courage is carried out in small everyday choices, choices which encourage you to seize the moment to change precisely *when* change is needed.

4. You Are Where You Are Supposed to Be

When times were difficult, I wanted to be anywhere other than where I was. It was hard for me to imagine the benefits that would come as the result of being where I was in life. Because I made intellectual interpretations without the influence of my heart, I questioned whether my interpretations were "correct." Once, during prayer and meditation, I asked for a sign on how to clearly interpret what I need to know. Later that night, I dreamt that a big, blue monster truck was on the road in front of me. The entire back window of the truck, where decals are normally posted, was covered in gigantic white letters that read, "OH BOY! I LOVE SCHOOL!!!" As I read the message, it was an obvious and unambiguous answer to my request. To drive the message of the dream even further home, the next morning, while I was driving Mckenna and Gavin to school, the license plate on a car in front of me read, "Lots to learn."

I looked at problems in my life as problems, instead of viewing them as instruments through which I can learn. The feeling tone of the dream was that Earth is a school and I can have a better attitude for learning. Wherever you are, you are where you are supposed to be, and the situation is there to help you grow, change, learn, and become. As you change, life as you know it changes. Knowing this and that all situations are temporary, be where you are. Just keep in mind that, even though you are where you are supposed to be, that does not mean you are meant to stay there.

CHAPTER EIGHT

WILLING TO BE VISIBLE

The reception security position was short-lived, as I knew it would be. I had other plans. Over the course of the months I worked in reception, I set and held the intention that an administrative position would open up. I continued to work four hours in accounting, getting to know the newly hired accounting manager, and also work the "security" shift three nights a week. During my evening shift, activity slowed down after 8:00 p.m., and I spent the time writing–drafting *The Sad, Sad Cloud*, my first children's book (Gavin's brainchild), and articles for Examiner. During the day, the new accounting manager and I developed a mutually respectful relationship, and after five months of working reception security, she offered me a full-time position as an accounting assistant. With forty hours a week, I could finally pay the rent in full and on time every month. It is a breath of fresh air with stabilizing financial relief for our housing situation, and more movement towards a new direction.

Although numbers are not exciting for me like they are for Matt, I've always identified with left-brain logic, which allows me to be exceptionally good at paperwork. With this position, I am excited to learn something new and enjoy the newfound work/life balance. The kids attend summer camp at the center, which means that, during the summer, they literally come to work with me five days a week. I love being in an environment conducive to personal growth with like-minded individuals. With weekly Sunday messages, and a variety of books in the bookstore, there is literary support as well as peer and congregational support. For the first year and a half of being a full-time employee, I am a kid in a candy store!

Then, one afternoon, a new employee is hired. Because I work in accounting, I often see sensitive financial and personal information. It comes with the job. However, on this particular day, I'm learning how to enter a new employee into the payroll system, which also requires entering the hourly rate.

I sit down beside the accounting manager, so I can see her computer screen. Before we begin, she says, "I just want to warn you. When you set up a new employee, you may see financial information that bothers you." I don't think anything of it. Then, I look back at the computer screen and see the huge disparity between what the new employee makes and what I make! I suddenly feel as if all the oxygen is leaving my body, like the air is being siphoned from the office. With what has to be deoxygenated blood flowing to my brain, disrupting my ability to focus on payroll instructions, I can barely concentrate. I take a deep breath, secretly gather my composure and mentally calculate a twenty-seven-dollar difference in our hourly wage. For the remainder of my shift, I am mentally worthless. I simply cannot concentrate on work, nor do I want to! Questions seize my attention. Who would have authorized this decision? How is this fair? What about integrity and equanimity? Is there a hierarchy *within* the spiritual center? When a reiterated part of the weekly Sunday message is that everyone has a significant contribution to make, is valuable, and contributes to the whole, how can there be such a discrepancy in pay for comparable administrative positions?

During my two and a half years of working in accounting, I periodically considered enrolling in UCLA Extension's Accounting Certificate Program. I was trying to convince myself I could stay in this line of work and grow to like numbers. I come in early, stay late, work on many weekends, and do my absolute best to honor my work so I can sleep well at night. This is precisely why I was asked to join the accounting department. I work from a place of integrity and service, and the accounting manager notices and appreciates it. She has grown to trust me, my judgment, and my ability to perform tasks that lure me out of my comfort zone (hence payroll). Now, I am entrusted to process extremely sensitive information and with that responsibility also comes "seeing information that may bother" me.

After three years of looking for work, wanting to be a part of something purposeful, jeopardizing already fragile communications with Dennis to follow through on what I felt called to do, investing myself within this spiritual community, and weathering financial issues *despite* a full-time position, I am devastated to observe a pay disparity that is fundamentally inconsistent with what is spoken during the Sunday message. I mean, It's not all about money, but then again, it *is* about the money. I did not see this coming. Am I bothered because the new employee may have asked for more, or that I am willing to accept so little? The spiritual center is not responsible for taking care of me. I am responsible for taking care of me. But how does the spiritual center decide for whom it will be a financial advocate? I understand job responsibilities vary in terms of the skill set required. However, I am perplexed as to how the value of what each employee contributes is determined. If I'm not willing to be my own advocate, to determine my value, then who will? In truth, the new employee has nothing to do with the fact that I accepted the wage I was offered, and not once spoke up for myself to ask for more. Yes, I have reason, but now, I can't help but wonder why I accept so little for myself, why I try to keep myself small by not going for what I really want. Just when I try to settle where I am not meant to settle, it becomes obvious my self-imposed comfort zone is an attempt to play it safe and remain who I have been. Yes, some things are meant to happen, but not all is meant to be.

Dennis isn't home with the kids. They must have stopped off somewhere after school. I can meditate! I hurry to get the pen and notebook from the bedside table, sit down on the living room floor with my legs crossed, back against the front of the sofa and open palms facing upwards. I am still in awe of how soothing silence is. There is something deeply restorative in simply being. The unimportant falls away and the real drifts in to be known. I begin again:

"I call upon my Higher Self to join me in my meditation. During this meditation, I ask that you protect me from any and all vibrations, energies, frequencies, and communications in all directions of time, past, present, and future, that are not of love, light, and the highest good. Please let this communication be clear. Let the answers be communicated to me in a way that is easy for me to understand. Please let me feel your loving energy when you are ready to begin. I thank you in advance for your presence." This is the guidance that comes through:

<u>Looking for it is also noticing that it's "not there."</u> *Fear is attempting to remain within you. It is trying to plant its roots within the impatience you feel toward the "movement" in your life. A reminder: When you think a positive thought followed by a negative thought, you negate the energy of movement and possibility. It's like cutting the roots before they've been implanted. There simply can be no growth. You want instant results, and you cannot understand why some things manifest instantaneously while others do not. Simply, what you believe and say with forceful energy ALWAYS manifests. Period. You are looking for proof that something is happening. Looking for it is also noticing that it's "not there." You know you have a place at the center, yet you're noticing the absence of your defined place. This halts the movement. Please, calm down. You are not sinking. You are STILL okay. Do not worry about time, your age, what you have "accomplished" through earthly calculations. You have undergone tremendous soul growth in the short amount of time you have been here. This is an accomplishment in and of itself. Embrace your inner, silent growth. You know where you have come from (pain, fear of abandonment, judgment, jealousy) to where you are now. It takes a lot of effort and strength to candidly look at oneself and make personal changes. Embrace your growth, your journey, your choices and yourself. You are loved.*

<u>You will know where and how to serve.</u> *Where are you to serve? You are serving right now by envisioning a world where all needs are met. You are serving when you exhibit acts of kindness, when you do for others unnecessarily, when you think kind thoughts and ask for the best outcome for all those involved. There are MANY ways to serve. Do not think that you are not of service without a specific title, income, position, or command. You serve your family, your community, the world around you, and your planet when you heal yourself and make space for love. You are serving. Please continue to serve in any manner you are called.*

The possibility to create greater discomfort or more of what you want. *With regard to basic needs being met (housing, education for children, paying your fair share), we told you that you would feel discomfort…great discomfort. This is because we knew when you felt the "weakest" in your life experience, or most compromised. You hoped for better, but you could not see farther than what was in front of you…more uncertainty and instability. So that is what you are living. We are not here to predict what will happen or what you must do. There are only possibilities of what could happen, given your beliefs, expectations, and energy. You have the possibility to create greater discomfort, or more of what you want. But the experience can only manifest what is able to come through you as a filter. Are you stopping your flow, or letting it flow? You feel that you are stopping your flow. We agree. Your fear body was VERY strong and it will not dissolve peacefully. You strengthen it with worry and doubt.*

We have seen what you have been able to create. You are capable of such greatness that you would surprise even yourself. And yes, you are right. Your world is quite small right now because you keep it small with worry about making a payment to someone. There are MUCH bigger ways of thinking. There are much bigger issues that need your attention, energy, and action. You have to let what is needed of you show itself. What you want for this world wants you to help bring it about. But the messages that seek expression through you are buried beneath your worry about making a payment. You are keeping your world small, when you so desperately want to expand. It's known as "getting in the way of yourself." Be who you are meant to be! So what if you have to make more adjustments in your life? So what if you have to travel the unknown road? You are calling yourself to be bigger; that is why you feel like you are "wasting time." It is never a waste, your soul is simply ready to do what it incarnated to do. Release the restrictions. Honor yourself. Honor your calling and rise to the occasion of growth. Your time has come.

Participate in your life. Have the experience to the fullest of your ability. Relax into life…into your life. There is no clock that you are racing against. There is only time in what you have created to remind you of dates, appointments, and worldly concerns. This is the only time that is recorded in your plane of existence, your world. In the larger picture, of all life, there is no time. There is only life and change. Life and change. Many of you hurry about life as if time is going someplace, running out. Time is ever-present. Yes, your earthly body will come to completion, BUT your soul remains and will simply pick up where it left off. Your soul will do exactly what it needs to do, exactly when it is ready to be done. Knowing this, you can relax. There is no need to "hurry up" and get it done, as if this is your only opportunity. You will have other opportunities. What we advise is that you have the experience to the fullest of your ability. Do not lean too much in one direction, such as worry, doubt, pleasure, the material, etc. Leaning too much in one direction throws you, your life experience, and your soul out of balance. You are here to experience many things and specific things. You are not here to dwell in one area for extended periods. When this happens and is continuous, you stagnate, and your soul feels lack…as if something is missing. Many of you have had this feeling of lack and longing that you are unable to quiet as long as you dwell and do not move as you are intended to. Movement, change, growth, service, and love is your goal. You have an inner thirst for this experience of giving, receiving, loving, and living. You cannot live (truly) without the other components of giving, receiving, and loving. When you are not in this place, you are dwelling where you are not meant to be, and every cell of your body will try to bring this to your attention.

With this piece of writing (book), you will impact many. Your words will encourage individuals across the world to walk authentically through life, to believe in what is in their hearts and what is trying to emerge. You will encourage many to believe that their life was meant to have a loving impact in and around their world. You will encourage many to "do for others more than you do for yourself." Many already feel this and want this but remain unsure of how to bring it about…just as you were unsure. Through the inspired act of writing down what has come through you (your being), you are at the cusp of making an impact, in the form of "throwing a pebble into a lake" that is ready for movement. You have to read the words that inspire and resonate within you the most. Different people perceive things differently. Sometimes some things have to be repeated until they are TRULY heard, absorbed, and (then) lived. Yours is an uncommon voice, and a necessary voice. Because many are thirsty for more love, compassion, generosity, kindness, and humanity in their life and in their world. Many are standing at the lake (edge) looking for the ripple effect that they are to keep moving. This is your stone (book). Throw it into the lake.

Weeks later, I am still posting articles on Examiner and, although my page views are increasing, I still don't *see* myself as a writer. I feel like a fraud, saying I am a writer while working in accounting. Roughly three weeks after the hourly-rate incident, I am sitting at my desk, feeling repurposed and scrolling through Facebook. To my surprise, the gentleman with whom I used to volunteer posts an event about a SuperSoul Session. I recognize the logo from Oprah Winfrey's Network because I *always* watch *SuperSoul Sunday* on OWN, so I click on the post. It reads:

> *This inspirational series featuring in-depth conversations between Oprah Winfrey and some of the most recognized spiritual thinkers of our time is coming to UCLA on September 12. The SuperSoul Sessions is the first live event as an extension of the* SuperSoul Sunday *TV show. This day-long event is free of charge, with an online form accepting entries for an opportunity to win tickets.*

Something in me shifts, and I don't recognize myself with the actions I take next. I have no intention of trying to win tickets. That's too "iffy." I stare at the post and with the firmest declaration of certainty, I say out loud, "I'm going to that!" From an unknown, but obviously clear, part of myself, I suddenly have the idea I will attend the event as a writer. I fervently Google OWN Network and SuperSoul Sessions to see what I can find. Within five minutes, I find the event press release, but I need an account to access the information, so I create one. Within one minute, I have access to the event network contacts. I sit at my desk, further ignoring my work, and craft an email for the two contacts listed on the press release. Something is truly moving me, because I am not playing around! I don't take one moment to stop and think of all the reasons I am not qualified, not *truly* a member of the press, or why I shouldn't send it . So I do it. I hit Send:

In response to the recent Facebook post for the SuperSoul Sessions to be held at Royce Hall on September 12, this event will serve as a "breath of fresh air" for those of us who crave inspirational and uplifting conversation. I am a professional Freelance Writer on Examiner.com and I would love to share your event with my audience through press coverage. My work includes writing as the National Spirituality Examiner with focus on spiritual growth, personal development, and spiritual documentaries. In exchange for press access, my coverage for the SuperSoul Sessions on Examiner will include the following:

- (First article) What makes the event unique and what I hope to learn.
- (Second article) Review of the speaker segment with an intent to capture the positive aspects.
- (Third article) A recap about the event as a whole, new perspectives and insights gained.

Please let me know if I can provide more information, or if you have any questions.

Thank you,
Bridgitte Jackson-Buckley

Within TEN minutes of my email, this is the Communications Director's response:

Hello Bridgitte,

Thank you so much for reaching out with interest in supporting the upcoming event. We are finalizing details now for the event overall, but we would love it if you could join us to observe and share your experience at the day-long event. We will have details to share in the next week or so regarding check-in.

Best,
C.~

I cannot believe my eyes! I am stunned, shocked, terrified, and excited all at the same time! I am actually going to be in the same building as Oprah Winfrey, presenting myself as a writer! What just happened?

Three days before the SuperSoul Session event, I post the first article, entitled *SuperSoul Sunday Comes to UCLA*, on Examiner. I am the only person who writes an article about the event, and on the day of SuperSoul Sessions, the article skyrockets on Examiner's trending list! That Saturday, after the first half of Sessions, the press are invited backstage for roundtable interviews. As we walk through the crowd, through the Green Room—"There's Deepak Chopra!!!"—and finally to the press room, three of us have the opportunity to remain backstage to interview Iyanla Vanzant and Elizabeth Gilbert.

As I wait for Ms. Vanzant to enter the room, I nervously shift my weight from side to side, hold onto my phone with both hands, to stop them from trembling, while texting my mother, as I look over my list of potential questions. To my surprise, the "hourly-rate-higher-than-mine" employee from the spiritual center walks into the press room. She is attending the event with a speaker from the spiritual center and is as surprised to see me as I am to see her! "Bridgitte, what are you doing here?" "My writing. I write on Examiner." "Oh," she says. I look back at my phone, praying she doesn't disclose that I actually work in accounting! "Stay strong," the text from my mother reads. I look up and Iyanla Vanzant walks into the room.

I write three articles for OWN for the SuperSoul Sessions event and they are "quite pleased with my coverage." Two weeks later, another Communications Director for OWN contacts me to see if I would "be interested in perhaps breaking the news about this new installment in the meditation series on Examiner.com" with an interview with Deepak Chopra! She writes, "I've very much enjoyed the articles you've written in support of OWN recently." One week later, I hold a telephone interview with Deepak Chopra and launch the start of the *21-Day Become What You Believe* Meditation Event!

"Follow the energy of where life is trying to lead you," I once heard Oprah say. I am getting more and more invitations to conduct interviews as my articles circulate online. About five months later, I am contacted by a publicist who mails a book entitled *The Book of Knowing and Worth*. I read the book and sit with the material for close to two weeks, when it hits me: "What you call to you is always a reflection of what you believe should be. And every time you say who you are, your world confirms." "Wait. What? All that shows up in my life is a direct result of what I believe I am *worthy* of having? The work I do at the spiritual center and the writing opportunities that come, or don't come, are results of what I *believe I am allowed* to have?" This message compels me to take a *thorough* look at what I believe can, or cannot, show up in my life, as well as what I am participating in the creation of on a larger scale. A part of me is reaching to write, while another part of me is trying to remain hidden and small. I have to decide which part of myself I will pay attention to. I love writing, but it is an unknown world I am unsure how to navigate. This accounting assistant position, is not what I want, but I can pay the rent. The truth of the matter is, if I really want to do something with writing, I have to own it. I have to stop this tuck-tail response of meekly saying, "I'm a writer," as if I don't really believe it. I have to accept that this is what I want to do, and have always wanted to do, but never believed in the possibility of it for myself. The past few months have shown me what is possible, what is within my reach, and what wants to happen through me. My job is to stop trying to hold it in; stop trying to sell myself the belief that good things only happen for other people. Lots of good things have happened for me. How many more "breadcrumbs" do I need to follow where the energy and my curiosity are trying to lead me? I'm only a "fraud" if I choose to believe I'm a fraud.

SUMMARY

1. To Look For It Is to Notice It's "Not There"

It is true, "The more you resist, the longer it persists." You cannot be afraid of a problem and yearn for a solution because the two cannot coexist in the same space. Until you first believe something to be true, you will not see it show up in your life. Your beliefs only allow you to see who or what you believe in. So when someone says, "Seeing is believing," it's actually the other way around. Believing is seeing.

2. You Will Know Where and How to Serve

Despite the fact that you may feel overwhelmed, pessimistic, or too busy to believe that any life other than the one you currently live is possible, there is a more expansive life trying to make itself available through you. The yearning for something vastly different is present because some part of you is reaching to live a life that uniquely defines who you are. This is why the yearning doesn't go away. For years, I tried to ignore the inner urge to write. I thought maybe it would just go away. Then, I found myself feeling like the biggest hypocrite when I would gloriously tell my children things like, "You can do anything you want to do. Just get a good education, work hard, and everything will be fine. All you have to do is believe in yourself." I wasn't even taking my own advice! There are many ways to serve, and many ways to be an example beyond giving empty advice you don't really believe. You can be of service in simply being who you truly are, when you give the advice you are now willing to live.

3. The Possibility to Create Greater Discomfort or More of What You Want

The first time I attended SuperSoul Sessions, and participated in the press roundtable, I was a nervous wreck. I worried the Communications Director would discover she had made a mistake and I was not supposed to be there. I participated in the interviews just fine, without any major display of being a novice, or stumbling over my words and questions, or behaving like a star-struck fan. But on the inside, I was filled with doubt. Here I was backstage, with many of the authors whose books I had read, and all I could think was, "I'm not supposed to be here." By the time I attended the third press roundtable at SuperSoul Sessions, there was no doubt in my mind that I was supposed to be there. It was no mistake. I was exactly where I was supposed to be. Other than the speaker line-up, the *only* thing that changed between the first SuperSoul Session event and the third was my perception of myself.

4. Participate in Your Life

After all the events, seminars, books, personal discussions, and good intentions, the one thing I can say I was missing was full commitment. Step by step, I moved out of the fear and away from the abyss of self-negating thoughts. I worked intently to move away from making choices which stem from a place of fear. And I made progress. Lots of progress. However, in all of my "moving-out-of," I cannot definitively say that I moved closer to full commitment. The lack of unyielding commitment to my writing demonstrated that, after all the inner work I had done, and after the moments of undeniable grace I had experienced, I still had the capacity to indulge doubt. It was like a tired relationship with an ex; you already know what you'll get will be disappointing, yet you entertain the idea of getting back together anyway. I made sincere attempts to be authentic, to make decisions and take actions I thought would help me to participate in the highest unfoldment of my life. But sometimes I missed. Sometimes I wanted to be afraid, uncertain, and filled with doubt. Why? Because for so long that was my uncomfortable comfort zone. I knew how to navigate that terrain. Just sit and worry all day, every day. Done. This, in fact, was the commitment I held true for years. But then, the more writing opportunities came my way, the more clear it became that my commitment had to shift. Doubting myself, worrying all day, and feeling like a fraud was not a commitment I could hold onto. It was time to make a different commitment, to participate in my life in a way I had not done before.

CHAPTER NINE

LIVING ON PURPOSE

"Hurry up! Get your stuff so we can go! We're going to be late," I say to Gavin while closing the lid on my coffee cup. "School is so boring," Gavin says. "Every time the teacher says we're going to do something new, I get excited, but then it's the same old stuff. It's the same thing every single day." I tighten the lid with regret that I understand how he feels. "I want to do something exciting and fun," he continues, "but it's always the same boring stuff." I look up from the cup and turn toward him, "I know, Gavin. I know exactly how you feel."

It's been over two and half years since I started working full-time in accounting. However, despite the arduous road to get here, I once again share a sentiment similar to Gavin's. Although I try to convince myself *this* work–good, steady, reliable accounting work–is work I can stay with, it is the same sentiment I've felt in every other administrative position I've held. I've been here before. Things go well for a period of time, while I'm preoccupied with learning something new; then, when the preoccupation wears off, I inevitably end up at the same point. No matter how much attention I pay to my work responsibilities, or how well I carry out tasks, an internal longing lingers below and fails to subside, even in the best of professional situations. Where is my professional place? Where do I belong if the professional structures I blend into consistently lead to discontent? I had hoped the spiritual center would be the place where I am meant to stay, my end result. But it is clear that it is not. I too want to spend my days doing something interesting and fulfilling. While Gavin is likely referring to "something exciting" like an African safari, I'm referring to what never stops calling to me.

The interviews and articles from the SuperSoul Sessions are helping to create more writing opportunities. With access to some of my favorite authors and spiritual leaders, I reach out for an interview, schedule the call early in the morning, before work, or drive home during my lunch break to conduct the interview. With the interviews and article views, I am moving higher in the ranks in the religion sector on Examiner and amazing myself at what I'm accomplishing! As a self-proclaimed lifelong learner, I still love to read books and have conversations to inquire about growth and expansion. I like the discussion and exchange of new ideas and insights beyond the text because I want to know. I want to learn what I can do to expand my growth and awareness, and how best to contribute to the expansion of those around me. When I engage in writing about subject matter that initiates spiritual intrigue, there is no underlying feeling that something is missing because nothing is missing. I am in my element. I'm no longer stifling and denying the vital expression of my true creative self. In accounting, as much as I enjoy working with the accounting manager, I am not in my element, and, like Gavin, I too want to get away. But let's be clear, I'm not referring to not being in my professional element as in temporary tedium. I'm referring to a chronic dissatisfaction and disconnection in my relationship with the work. Due to responsibilities, financial security is a viable reason to remain in a job, even if you're not in your element. I, of all people, understand the position of being scared of the uncertainty you face without a secure job. Working a job you dislike to gain financial security is a sacrifice worth making, and you have to think carefully before you put financial responsibilities on the line. However, each time I do this, after a period of time, I inevitably begin to feel like each day contributes to the gradual loss of a part of myself. Even though there are days when it is difficult to express an idea on paper the way I imagine it, I enjoy the challenge of writing to create practical ways to say what I'm inspired to say. Writing is the non-conformist path in which I can get away, go to another place to explore ways to express ideas. So when I sit at my accounting desk and think, "If I have to do this for another five years, I can die right now," it's time to get away; it's time for me to step away.

Thank goodness the spiritual center is exactly as it is. In being here, I have deepened my spiritual practice, clarified who I am, where I want to be, and what I want to do. The loss of the house, the strain on my marriage, the argument with Rachel, the pay disparity, accepting so little for myself, and even the realization that the spiritual center is not my end result have all contributed to the gradual "burning away" of pervasive feelings of anger, self-doubt, fear, and unworthiness. I am grateful. If there is one truth I've learned it, is this: The expansion of awareness is not about getting something, it's about letting go of what is no longer necessary. *Everything* serves a purpose to contribute to the phoenix rising from the ashes.

There's no magic formula, no magic fairy dust. *You have arrived at the understanding that NOT ONE circumstance will leave your daily experience until you have had enough of it; until you believe you are well; until you believe you are worthy and capable of more; until you forgive yourself for "past mistakes;" until love and service are a priority in your life. That's it. No, there's no magic formula, no magic fairy dust. There is YOU... the problem, yet you are also the solution. The catch is that you cannot solve any problem from your normal way of thinking that created the problem. You have to interject hope where there was despair, faith where there was fear, love where there was anger, and service where there was always taking without giving back. Life is beautiful, because throughout the journey of your life, you are born into love, lose sight of this love, and eventually reconnect with this love. Amidst the reconnection, you begin to grow, to understand, to know that love is simply the only answer. Love is all there is, you have but to welcome it into your experience. "If nobody has done it (within your world), maybe it IS for you to do." This is a place where you can begin.*

The idea must pass through you into the open world. *For as you, and others, begin to see that they have a lot to offer beyond money, this will begin the ripple effect of reclaiming personal power. You have the power to use your voice so that the other person who is listening hears you and moves closer to you. Another person will hear and see the two of you and begin to listen attentively because she also wants to help, but hasn't known how. Trust what is trying to emerge EVEN IF it seems completely out of your realm of action. The authenticity of how intense the inspiration is has verified within you that the idea must pass through you into the open world. This is not beyond you, because as you say "yes" to service, love, generosity, and compassion, life will say "yes" to the path you are on. Life will show you the way. Life is the way because YOU are the way. Let yourself be the conduit, the vessel, the passageway through which others see a path to self-healing, self-empowerment, brotherly and sisterly compassion, and the regeneration of humanity in your world. You are the change that is necessary. You ARE the one, the thing, the miracle, the catalyst that you have been waiting for...YOU. Love to you.*

Besides the early-morning cleaning crew, I'm the first one in today. The accounting manager often arrives before me, but today she is later than usual. I settle in to check my emails and voicemails while I wait for her to arrive. When we first met three years ago, I never anticipated that she would become one of my dearest friends, having made a profound impact on my life. Sometimes people around you see qualities in you that you cannot yet see for yourself. They recognize and acknowledge your potential, capabilities, and strengths. As much as I insisted that I was not the person to take on the responsibility of payroll, she believed in me when I was incredibly reluctant to move out of my comfort zone. With her compassionate encouragement, the experience of working with her gently stretched me to see that I'm capable of more than I've allowed. On a daily basis, I watch her deal with professional pressure, a heavy workload, intricate financial details, and staff management in the most graceful and loving way. Within stressful situations, she provides a beautiful example of how to work collaboratively with others from a place of conscious leadership. I have tremendous respect and admiration for her, and if I'm ever in a position to lead others, it is her example I will follow.

Just as I log into my email, there is a faint knock on my office door. It's Joan, the accounting manager. She opens the door and carefully walks in as to not disturb me. "Hi Bridgitte," she says and closes the door behind her. After three years of working here, when a staff member closes the door after entering, I know that something interesting is about to be disclosed. "Good morning," I say as she moves closer to my desk. "I need to talk to you," she says. My eyebrows raise, as if to say, "Tell me more!" Yet, I say nothing. "I've submitted my resignation. The twenty-fifth of this month will be my last day." I remain silent, mentally displaced as ambivalence floods my mind. "She's leaving! Oh wow! It's over." My working relationship with Joan is one of the main reasons I've remained at the spiritual center. Without Joan's presence, there will be no buffer between me and the chronic dissatisfaction of this position. In her absence, I will most likely be asked to take over some of her job responsibilities and most likely (once again) try to convince myself to stay on a path I want to get off. I'll start to make a *little* more money and, once that happens, it will be even harder to let go. This will lead me farther away from where I want to go. I take a few days to let the news of her resignation sink in and come to the conclusion that *this is a moment*, my moment to, once and for all, decide on my direction. Follow the energy of where love is trying to lead you, echoes in my thoughts. I can no longer think of a reason *not* to follow the energy of where life is trying to lead me to reconnect with love. One week later, I submit my own letter of resignation.

Take another step. *Each and every time you thought you could not go on, that you would not be able to go on, or that you would simply give up…you continued to take another step. You continued to keep breathing, to keep contemplating, and you continue to keep asking where you are needed. There must be movement within in order to spur movement without. Ride the flow and feel that it will carry you, is carrying you, to where you need to be. Trust the process. Trust the journey and know that, as your life opens up to movement, your spirit feels life and inspiration once again. Listen to what you are telling YOU. Listen without judgment, without intellectual caution, and without intellectual hesitation. Listen with an open, unguarded heart and TRUST your soul's connection to the vastness of life. Life is trying to make its way through you, so you must open yourself up to be led. It is in being led by your heart that you will meet your True Self.*

<u>Know without needing validation.</u> *You are walking to the stone down the road. Your stone will not move unless you decide to change your direction. You will not make haste. You will not "hurry it along." You will arrive at the precise moment your stone is ready to receive you. You may not know (in your head) where you are going, but you can feel in your body that the direction is in alignment to your soul's purpose. Know without needing validation. Quiet your mind. Hold no worries. Meditate in stillness. Be who you are in love. Be the love you wish to see in the world.*

What is my life's purpose?

To write, communicate, and deliver messages.

What message/s am I to deliver?

The process and journey of your spiritual journey: the growth, transformation, difficulty, doubts, and grace.

What is trying to emerge through me, as me, from this situation?

The experience that is within you needs to be shared with others because you are the message. Your experience is the catalyst for others.

How can my experience be the catalyst for others when I don't know how this ends?

It is not about "the end result." It is about the experience within the journey... the journey that leads to growth, transformation, and change.

The above meditation took place in April 2012, four years before I left the spiritual center. When the above guidance came through, the idea of writing, communicating, and delivering messages seemed unreachable, distant, and unrelated to the events taking place in my life. Now, there is no longer doubt or uncertainty in seeing myself as a writer with many possibilities available to me. I *know* they are available and within reach. All that I have wanted for my life and for my writing feels possible, because it *is* possible. Knowing this makes everything easier. I no longer believe I have to *make* things happen, direct the flow of events, or try to control timing. I can let things happen by consciously showing up through inspired action, knowing without needing validation, and realizing I AM the *"magic fairy dust."*

Roughly six months before I resigned from the spiritual center, I moved into my own office. However, I did not decorate it with one personal item. At that time, I knew there was no need to get comfortable. Something in me knew my days were numbered. Even when the new bookkeeper was hired into our department, six months before I resigned, instead of merely "showing her the ropes," I *knew* I was training her as my replacement. That is precisely what I told myself each time I trained her on an accounting process.

On March 4, my final day at the spiritual center, I say goodbye to my friend's on staff. And, for the last time, I say goodbye to acquiescing to be out of alignment with my soul's purpose. I am under no impression that going forward as a full-time writer will be easy, but I am willing to try. I continue with Examiner and writing on behalf of OWN. One month later, I attend the third SuperSoul Sessions event and once again participate in the press roundtable interviews. This time, I sit across from Gary Zukav, Gabrielle Bernstein, Angela Davis, Pastor John Gray, Wes Moore, and Glennon Doyle-Metlon, and ask my questions as if we are old acquaintances. With my mother standing at the back of the room, there is no need for her to send another "be strong" text. I *am* being strong. I am being me, and there is no doubt in my mind that I'm supposed to be here.

Since leaving the spiritual center, I set the intention to draw specific individuals into my life for professional endeavors. At night, after meditation, I lie on the bed and envision pure white light coming up from the center of the earth, through the bottom of my feet, extending all the way up through the top of my head. I envision the light extending up like a lighthouse beacon shining over the city. With deep sincerity, I honestly articulate experiences I want to participate in and call individuals into my life through what I refer to as a Soul Call.

While I envision the light extending up from the top of my head like a lighthouse beacon, I say the following:

"In the highest perfection, I am calling out to all souls of integrity, authenticity, creativity, and sincerity who would like to work with me and are interested in creating high-level articles, books, documentaries, screenplays, projects, and initiatives that contribute to the rise of consciousness on the planet. Let these souls find me by whatever means, let them hire me for well-paid work, let us collaborate together toward creative solutions for what is needed and what is wanted. I ask that these individuals and these experiences find me quickly, lovingly, and gently. And in the highest perfection, let us all be blessed. Thank you."

A few months later, while conducting a telephone interview with Eiman Al Zaabi, author of *The Art of Surrender*, I am amazed at the amount of material in her book. I ask where the information came from. She responds, "I channeled a lot of it." Before she can complete her sentence, I think, "I have some material maybe I can use for a book!" It has been years since I looked over the guidance from my meditation sessions. My meditations now consist of prolonged silence and prayer for the well-being of others and for continual clarity for myself. I still have questions, of course, but not like I used to. I know everything is working out for my highest good, but it's not just words now. It's real. In addition to now writing for Gaia, Patheos, and Medium, and submitting queries to magazines, I am inspired by my conversation with Eiman. I have a persistent feeling that I should type the meditation guidance into Microsoft Word. I work on this for several months and begin to add stories of what went on throughout the period of the recorded meditations. I don't know what will happen when I finish typing the guidance, but, like the persistent feeling I had to volunteer and to write, it feels like it should be done now. I also have a relationship with several publicists, and there is one in particular I continue to have a thought that I should ask if she knows a literary agent. I have had enough experience with internal prompts by now to know that, when a thought prompts me to take action and does not go away, it is not to be ignored.

I send the publicist an email and ask about an agent. I'm not expecting anything. My intention is to follow through on the internal prompt without attachment to an outcome. She emails back and says, "Let's talk on Tuesday." Tuesday arrives and I call the publicist. After pleasantries, she informs me she was planning to tell me it's difficult to get a literary agent if you don't have a built-in audience and large social media following. I don't have either of those. Four months after I left the spiritual center, Examiner shut down operations and closed down the website. I did not have access to log in to write a final article to inform my subscribers where they could find my content. However, I didn't see this as a problem, just a shift in direction. But on the telephone call with the publicist, she informs me that, after I sent the email, she met a new literary agent. Imagine that. During our conversation, she offers to introduce me to the literary agent, but will first have to contact her, and will get back to me.

I say thank you and we hang up. Ten minutes later the publicist calls me back. "Bridgitte! You are not going to believe who called me as soon as you and I got off the phone!" "Who?!" I ask with delight. "The literary agent I told you about! Do you mind if I give her your contact information?" "Hell no!" I say. The publicist does a virtual introduction and the next day the literary agent and I talk. After a forty-five-minute telephone conversation, it's clear we have good chemistry. She asks me to send over a draft proposal of what I have prepared. I'm nervous at this point. This is so unexpected, but a welcome surprise. It takes two weeks for me to complete the draft proposal. One month later, the literary agent contacts me to discuss the proposal. I am a nervous wreck. What if she doesn't like it? Then what? What if she *does* like it? Then what? Dennis tells me to calm down, because, after all, this is what I say I want. We schedule a time to talk and, during the telephone conversation, the literary agent says, "I'd love to work with you."

Writing a book is something I've wanted to do for the majority of my life. When the opportunity to write a book appeared, it also brought with it an unexpected anxiety toward change and the fear of failure. Although it is something I have wanted to do, when the opportunity surfaced, so did the fear of the change it would bring. I was afraid of the unknowns and of not rising to the occasion. For example, the week I sit down to write Chapter Three to include in the book proposal, out of nowhere I experience a terrible pain in my left shoulder. The pain is so excruciating I cannot lift my arm, lie on either side of my body, or move my arm in any direction. Prior to the onset of the shoulder pain, I did not sprain my shoulder, I did not lift anything heavy, nor did I fall. Yet, a few days after a conversation with my literary agent, the pain of a frozen shoulder emerges.

During our conversation, my literary agent tells me she needs three solid chapters in the book proposal to send out to potential buyers. Of course, I am excited to hear this! However, I am equally nervous. While thinking about completing Chapter Three, I worry about my writing, how the book will be received, how my life will change in unanticipated ways, and whether I will lose all anonymity.

Not only does my frozen shoulder represent a psychosomatic response to my internal conflict and self-imposed stress, it also represents the fear I hold toward imminent change making its way into my life.

Perhaps you would like to think there is an end to change, but there isn't. Change is an intricate and vital part of life that asks you, and me, to begin again and again, to reorient yourself. When change happens in your life, because you don't know what is going to happen, you may also experience the "frozen shoulder." However, you cannot let the "frozen shoulder" or fear of change stop you from moving forward, just as I could not and did not. Within a few hours of a candid conversation with a close friend, of voicing out loud what lies beneath my fears, the pain in my shoulder begins to dissipate. By the next morning, the pain is completely gone.

The good thing about my frozen-shoulder episode is that I talked with a trusted friend to quickly identify and verbalize the emotional trigger of what change represents in this particular situation.

The shoulder pain/fear serves as an opportunity to acknowledge the spiritual and personal growth I've made. At an earlier time, I would have let fear propel me into a state of despair for weeks. As you move along the path of growth and change, you will notice fear becomes less debilitating. It may momentarily knock you off balance, but as you become adept at identifying what lies beneath, you can quickly return to balance.

You can learn to move with the change with ease and grace, without beating yourself up or running away from what scares you. You can choose to accept what is trying to come to you, even if you're not sure what it is or where it will lead you.

Before I email the final proposal to the literary agent to send to potential buyers, I say the following prayer before I hit SEND:

I stand in faith

I walk in courage

I am not afraid

Because I am not alone.

In December 2017, my first book, *The Gift of Crisis: How I Used Meditation to Go from Financial Failure to a Life of Purpose* is contracted to be published.

The gift of crisis is the opportunity to connect with a greater consciousness to prepare yourself for transformation, to see with new eyes, to grow with fluidity, and to ultimately ask:

Who will I become when I no longer make choices to avoid something, but instead make choices from love to create something? When my actions and choices are rooted in truth? My *own* truth, when what I say, what I do, and what I believe are in complete harmony. Who will I allow myself to become when I recognize *I AM Divine*?

EPILOGUE

It isn't until eight years after the loss of the house, when I begin to write Chapter One and need Dennis' input on the work he did on the house, that, for the first time, we look at photos of what was once our home. Only Dennis knew how hard it was for me to lose the house on forty-first, just as only I knew how hard it was for him. As we look at the online photos of my childhood home, the house he renovated for his family, we share a silent and intimate moment in knowing we survived it. We've come out on the other side where something was lost, yet so much was gained. We moved beyond the loss of the house, and now sit with an unspoken but shared understanding that we have forgiven ourselves and each other. We have passed many days together letting go and turning within. In this new place of beginning again, the depth of tender resilience will forever reside and hold a loving space between us.

ACKNOWLEDGMENTS

To my husband, Dennis Buckley. For encouraging me to choose faith over fear to "do my own thing."

To my children, Greyson, Mckenna, and Gavin Buckley. For helping me to expand my capacity to give and receive love and *be* with my heart.

To my parents, Matthew and Bobbie Butler. You are the definition of unconditional love and all I aspire to become.

To Nikki Gilbert, Lisa Johnson-Woods, Anny Liu, and Chris Hubert. Your friendship contributes more to my life than you will ever know.

To Christopher Butler, Kaori Takagi, and Nandini Kishori. For the consistent question, "How is the book coming along?" Your interest *was* encouragement! Thank you.

To my literary agent, Priya Doraswamy. For patience, guidance, and the foresight of what this book could be and for being a wonderful example of women supporting women.

To Chris McKenney, Brenda Knight, and Mango Publishing. For the creative vision to see possibilities where others did not.

To Mango Publishing's Design and Marketing team. For the beautiful book cover and banner. Thank you.

To Kimberly Meredith. For the many ways your presence in my life contributes to love, transformation, and growth.

To Beth Grossman. For introducing me to Priya Doraswamy *and* Kimberly Meredith.

To the authors of my favorite books. For writing that is honest, interested in making a difference and inspires me to do for others what was done for me.

To employees of the Culver City Julian Dixon Library and the Playa Vista Branch of the Los Angeles Public Library. For patience, assistance, and never asking why I visit the library so often!

And to my writing group, Roxanne Reaver, April Rivera, and Catherine Hammons. "Be grateful for whoever comes, because each has been sent as a guide from beyond," (Rumi). It was clear from the beginning I was not meant to complete this book without you. Your presence provided an honest space to explore and write about spiritual concepts in a loving and practical way. Your sincere and valuable input was consistently in alignment with the highest vision for the book. You are the quintessential examples of love, grace, authentic creativity, and service to others beyond self. I am deeply grateful for you.

ABOUT THE AUTHOR

Bridgitte Jackson-Buckley

Bridgitte Jackson-Buckley, born in Los Angeles, CA in 1971, is an American author, blogger, memoirist, and interviewer. As an only child for sixteen years, Bridgitte loved to read beyond her skill level. She always carried a pocket dictionary while reading Stephen King books. Displaying a natural talent for writing in her youth, Bridgitte has been writing in journals since she was in the fourth grade. During college, Bridgitte moved away from writing to pursue a "practical and safe" career in medicine. Several years later, and after a variety of occupations, Bridgitte returned to her first love–writing–and quickly became known for in-depth articles on leading New Thought luminaries such as: Eckhart Tolle, Iyanla Vanzant, Deepak Chopra, Radhanath Swami, Elizabeth Gilbert, Penney Peirce, Elizabeth Lesser, Paul Selig, Marie Forleo, and several others including American singer, songwriter and guitarist Trevor Hall.

As a freelance writer, Bridgitte has written online articles for Examiner, Tiny Buddha, Recreate Your Life Story, Medium, Patheos, Thrive Global, and Gaia. She was the lead writer in launching Oprah Winfrey Network's Super Soul Sunday website, the "21-Day Become What You Believe Meditation and Seven Days to Restful Sleep for "Oprah & Deepak's Guide to Whole Health" in addition to various articles for Super Soul Sessions I–III. With a writing focus that includes spirituality, change, challenge, and transformation, Bridgitte's writing unexpectedly draws readers inward through her ability to convey complex spiritual concepts in a practical and accessible style.

Bridgitte's educational background includes a BA in psychology from the University of California, Berkeley, and the United States Peace Corps, both which have given her a broad base from which to approach many topics. Being bilingual, Bridgitte has traveled extensively throughout Central America including Belize, Costa Rica, El Salvador, Guatemala, Honduras, and Nicaragua from which much of her travel writing is based upon. Additional travels include Hong Kong, Malaysia, and Thailand.

Bridgitte now resides in Los Angeles with her husband, three children, and Miniature Schnauzer, and enjoys working with individuals and organizations who are interested in conscious change, conscious business practices, and conscious leadership and empowerment.

CPSIA information can be obtained
at www.ICGtesting.com
Printed in the USA
BVHW07s1334021018
529049BV00001B/1/P

9 781633 537941